Second Grand Challenge and Workshop on Multimodal Language (Challenge-HML 2020)

Online
10 July 2020

ISBN: 978-1-7138-1377-4

ACL 2020

**The 58th Annual Meeting of the
Association for Computational Linguistics**

**Proceedings of the Second Grand Challenge and Workshop
on Multimodal Language (Challenge-HML)**

July 10, 2020
Online (due to COVID-19 pandemic)

Introduction

The Second Grand-Challenge and Workshop on Multimodal Language (Challenge-HML) offers a unique opportunity for interdisciplinary researchers to study and model interactions between modalities of language, vision, and acoustic. This is the continuation of the Challenge-HML at ACL 2018. Modeling multimodal language is a growing research area in NLP. This research area pushes the boundaries of multimodal learning and requires advanced neural modeling of all three constituent modalities. Advances in this research area allow the field of NLP to take the leap towards better generalization to real-world communication (as opposed to limitation to textual applications), and better downstream performance in Conversational AI, Virtual Reality, Robotics, HCI, Healthcare, and Education.

Organizers:

Amir Zadeh, Language Technologies Institute, Carnegie Mellon University
Louis-Philippe Morency, Language Technologies Institute, Carnegie Mellon University
Paul Pu Liang, Machine Learning Department, Carnegie Mellon University
Soujanya Poria, Singapore University of Technology and Design

Invited Speakers:

Rada Mihalcea, University of Michigan (USA)
Ruslan Salakhutdinov, Carnegie Mellon University (USA)
M. Ehsan Hoque, University of Rochester (USA)
Yejin Choii, Washington University (USA)

Table of Contents

A Transformer-based joint-encoding for Emotion Recognition and Sentiment Analysis

Jean-Benoit Delbrouck and **Noé Tits** and **Mathilde Brousmiche** and **Stéphane Dupont**
Information, Signal and Artificial Intelligence Lab
University of Mons, Belgium
{jean-benoit.delbrouck, noe.tits, mathilde.brousmiche, stephane.dupont}@umons.ac.be

Abstract

Understanding expressed sentiment and emotions are two crucial factors in human multimodal language. This paper describes a Transformer-based joint-encoding (TBJE) for the task of Emotion Recognition and Sentiment Analysis. In addition to use the Transformer architecture, our approach relies on a modular co-attention and a glimpse layer to jointly encode one or more modalities. The proposed solution has also been submitted to the ACL20: Second Grand-Challenge on Multimodal Language to be evaluated on the CMU-MOSEI dataset. The code to replicate the presented experiments is open-source [1].

1 Introduction

Predicting affective states from multimedia is a challenging task. Emotion recognition task has existed working on different types of signals, typically audio, video and text. Deep Learning techniques allow the development of novel paradigms to use these different signals in one model to leverage joint information extraction from different sources. This paper aims to bring a solution based on ideas taken from Machine Translation (Transformers, Vaswani et al. (2017)) and Visual Question Answering (Modular co-attention, Yu et al. (2019)). Our contribution is not only very computationally efficient, it is also a viable solution for Sentiment Analysis and Emotion Recognition. Our results can compare with, and sometimes surpass, the current state-of-the-art for both tasks on the CMU-MOSEI dataset (Zadeh et al., 2018b).

This paper is structured as follows: first, in section 2, we quickly go over the related work that have been evaluated on the MOSEI dataset, we then proceed to describe our model in Section 3, we then explain how we extract our modality features from raw videos in Section 4 and finally, we present the dataset used for our experiments and their respective results in section 5 and 6.

2 Related work

Over the years, many creative solutions have been proposed by the research community in the field of Sentiment Analysis and Emotion Recognition. In this section, we proceed to describe different models that have been evaluated on the CMU-MOSEI dataset. To the best of our knowledge, none of these ideas uses a Tansformer-based solution.

The Memory Fusion Network (MFN, Zadeh et al. (2018a)) synchronizes multimodal sequences using a multi-view gated memory that stores intraview and cross-view interactions through time.

Graph-MFN (Zadeh et al., 2018b) consists of a Dynamic Fusion Graph (DFG) built upon MFN. DFG is a fusion technique that tackles the nature of cross-modal dynamics in multimodal language. The fusion is a network that learns to models the n-modal interactions and can dynamically alter its structure to choose the proper fusion graph based on the importance of each n-modal dynamics during inference.

Sahay et al. (2018) use Tensor Fusion Network (TFN), i.e. an outer product of the modalities. This operation can be performed either on a whole sequence or frame by frame. The first one lead to an exponential increase of the feature space when modalities are added that is computationally ex-pensive. The second approach was thus preferred. They showed an improvement over an

---

[1] https://github.com/jbdel/MOSEI_UMONS

1

Proceedings of the 58th Annual Meeting of the Association for Computational Linguistics, pages 1–7
Seattle, USA, July5 - 10, 2020. ©2017 Association for Computational Linguistics
https://doi.org/10.18653/v1/P17

early fusion baseline.

Recently, Shenoy and Sardana (2020) propose a solution based on a context-aware RNN, Multilogue-Net, for Multi-modal Emotion Detection and Sentiment Analysis in conversation.

3 Model

This section aims to describe the two model variants evaluated in our experiment: a monomodal variant and a multimodal variant. The monomodal variant is used to classify emotions and sentiments based solely on L (Linguistic), on V (Visual) or on A (Acoustic). The multimodal version is used for any combination of modalities.

Our model is based on the Transformer model (Vaswani et al., 2017), a new encoding architecture that fully eschews recurrence for sequence encoding and instead relies entirely on an attention mechanism and Feed-Forward Neural Networks (FFN) to draw global dependencies between input and output. The Transformer allows for significantly more parallelization compared to the Recurrent Neural Network (RNN) that generates a sequence of hidden states h_t, as a function of the previous hidden state h_{t-1} and the input for position t.

3.1 Monomodal Transformer Encoding

The monomodal encoder is composed of a stack of B identical blocks but with their own set of training parameters. Each block has two sub-layers. There is a residual connection around each of the two sub-layers, followed by layer normalization (Ba et al., 2016). The output of each sub-layer can be written like this:

$$\text{LayerNorm}(x + \text{Sublayer}(x)) \qquad (1)$$

where Sublayer(x) is the function implemented by the sub-layer itself. In traditional Transformers, the two sub-layers are respectively a multi-head self-attention mechanism and a simple Multi-Layer Perceptron (MLP).

The attention mechanism consists of a Key K and Query Q that interacts together to output a attention map applied to Context C:

$$\text{Attention}(Q, K, C) = \text{softmax}(\frac{QK^\top}{\sqrt{k}})C \qquad (2)$$

In the case of self-attention, K, Q and C are the same input. If this input is of size $N \times k$, the operation $QK^\top$ results in a squared attention matrix containing the affinity between each row N. Expression $\sqrt{k}$ is a scaling factor. The multi-head attention (MHA) is the idea of stacking several self-attention attending the information from different representation sub-spaces at different positions:

$$\text{MHA}(Q, K, C) = \text{Concat}(\text{head}_1, ..., \text{head}_h)W_o$$

$$\text{where head}_i = \text{Attention}(QW_i^Q, KW_i^K, CW_i^C) \qquad (3)$$

A subspace is defined as slice of the feature dimension k. In the case of four heads, a slice would be of size $\frac{k}{4}$. The idea is to produce different sets of attention weights for different feature sub-spaces. After encoding through the blocks, output $\tilde{x}$ can be used by a projection layer for classification. In Figure 1, x can be any modality feature as described in Section 4.

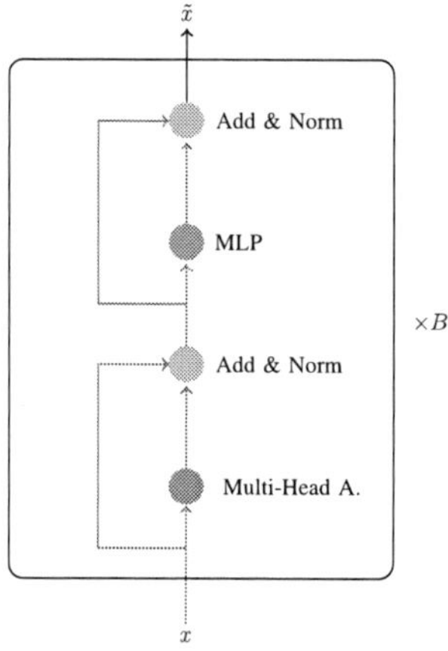

Figure 1: Monomodal Transformer encoder.

3.2 Multimodal Transformer Encoding

The idea of a multimodal transformer consists in adding a dedicated transformer (section 3.1) for each modality we work with. While our contribution follows this procedure, we also propose three ideas to enhance it: a joint-encoding, a modular co-attention (Yu et al., 2019) and a glimpse layer at the end of each block.

The modular co-attention consists of modulating the self-attention of a modality, let's call it y, by a primary modality x. To do so, we switch the key K and context C of the self-attention from y to

x. The operation $QK^\top$ results in an attention map that acts like an affinity matrix between the rows of modality matrix x and y. This computed alignment is applied over the context C (now x) and finally we add the residual connection y. The following equation describes the new attention sub-layer:

$$y = \text{LayerNorm}(y + \text{MHA}(y, x, x)) \qquad (4)$$

In this scenario, for the operation $QK^\top$ to work as well as the residual connection (the addition), the feature sizes of x and y must be equal. This can be adjusted with the different transformation matrices of the MHA module. Because the encoding is joint, each modality is encoded at the same time (i.e. we don't unroll the encoding blocks for one modality before moving on to another modality). This way, the MHA attention of modality y for block b is done by the representation of x at block b.

Finally, we add a last layer at the end of each modality block, called the glimpse layer, where the modality is projected in a new space of representation. A glimpse layer consists of stacking G soft attention layers and stacking their outputs. Each soft attention is seen as a glimpse. Formally, we define the soft attention (SoA) i with input matrix $M \in \mathbb{R}^{N \times k}$ by a MLP and a weighted sum:

$$a_i = \text{softmax}(v_i^{a\top}(W_m M))$$
$$\text{SoA}_i(M) = m_i = \sum_{j=0}^{N} a_{ij} M_j \qquad (5)$$

where W_m if a transformation matrix of size $2k \times k$, v_i^a is of size $1 \times 2k$ and m_i a vector of size k. Then we can define the glimpse mechanism for matrix M of glimpse size G^m as the stacking of all glimpses:

$$\mathbf{G}_M = \text{Stacking}(m_1, \ldots, m_{G^m})$$

Note that before the parameter W_m, whose role is to embed the matrix M in a higher dimension, is shared between all glimpses (this operation is therefore only computed once) while the set of vectors $\{v_i^a\}$ computing the attention weights from this bigger space is dedicated for each glimpse. In our contribution, we always chose $G^m = N$ so the sizes allow us to perform a final residual connections $M = \text{LayerNorm}(M + \mathbf{G}_M)$.

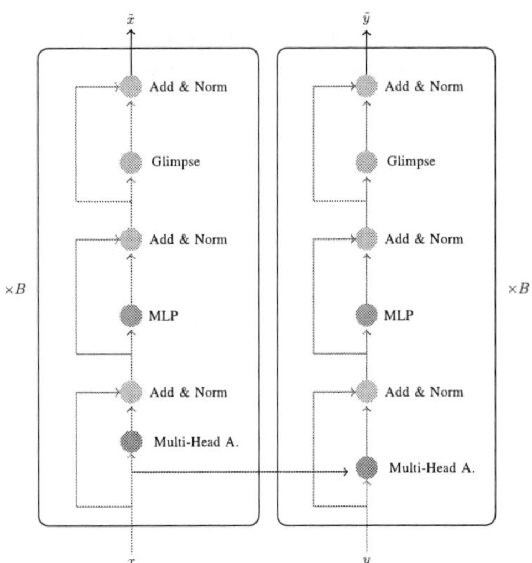

Figure 2: Multimodal Transformer Encoder for two modalities with joint-encoding.

The Figure 2 depicts the encoding for two features where modality x is modulating the modality y. This encoding can be ported to any number of modalities by duplicating the architecture. In our case, it is always the linguistic modality that modulates the others.

3.3   Classification layer

After all the Transformer blocks were computed, a modality goes into a final glimpse layer of size 1. The result is therefore only one vector. The vectors of each modality are summed element-wise, let's call the results of this sum s, and are then projected over possible answers according to the following equation:

$$y \sim p = W_a(\text{LayerNorm}(s)) \qquad (6)$$

If there is only one modality, the sum operation is omitted.

4   Feature extractions

This section aims to explain how we pre-compute the features for each modality. These features are the inputs of the Transformer blocks. Note that the features extraction is done independently for each example of the dataset.

4.1   Linguistic

Each utterance is tokenized and lowercase. We also remove special characters and punctuation. We build our vocabulary against the train-set and end up with a glossary of 14.176 unique words. We embed each word in a vector of 300 dimensions using GloVe (Pennington et al., 2014). If a word from the validation or test-set is not in present our vocabulary, we replace it with the unknown token "unk".

4.2 Acoustic

The acoustic part of the signal of the video contains a lot of speech. Speech is used in conversations to communicate information with words but also contains a lot of information that are non linguistic such as nonverbal expressions (laughs, breaths, sighs) and prosody features (intonation, speaking rate). These are important data in an emotion recognition task.

Acoustic features widely use in the speech processing field such as F0, formants, MFCCs, spectral slopes consist of handcrafted sets of high-level features that are useful when an interpretation is needed, but generally discard a lot of information. Instead, we decide to use low-level features for speech recognition and synthesis, the mel-spectrograms. Since the breakthrough of deep learning systems, the mel-spectrograms have become a suitable choice.

The spectrum of a signal is obtained with Fourier analysis that decompose a signal in a sum of sinusoids. The amplitudes of the sinusoids constitute the amplitude spectrum. A spectrogram is the concatenation over time of spectra of windows of the signal. Mel-spectrogram is a compressed version of spectrograms, using the fact the human ear is more sensitive to low frequencies than high frequencies. This representation thus attributes more resolution for low frequencies than high frequencies using mel filter banks. A mel-spectrogram is typically used as an intermediate step for text-to-speech synthesis (Tachibana et al., 2018) in state-of-the-art systems as audio representation, so we believe it is a good compromise between dimensionality and representation capacity.

Our mel-spectrograms were extracted with the same procedure as in (Tachibana et al., 2018) with librosa (McFee et al., 2015) library with 80 filter banks (the embedding size is therefore 80). A tem-poral reduction by selecting one frame every 16 frames was the applied.

4.3 Visual

Inspired by the success of convolutional neural networks (CNNs) in different tasks, we chose to extract visual features with a pre-trained CNN. Current models for video classification use CNNs with 3D convolutional kernels to process the temporal information of the video together with spatial information (Tran et al., 2015). The 3D CNNs learn spatio-temporal features but are much more expensive than 2D CNNs and prone to overfitting. To reduce complexity, Tran et al. (2018) explicitly factorizes 3D convolution into two separate and successive operations, a 2D spatial convolution and a 1D temporal convolution. We chose this model, named R(2+1)D-152, to extract video features for the emotion recognition task. The model is pretrained on Sports-1M and Kinetics.

The model takes as input a clip of 32 RGB frames of the video. Each frame is scaled to the size of 128 x 171 and then cropped a window of size 112 x 112. The features are extracted by taking the output of the spatiotemporal pooling. The feature vector for the entire video is obtained by sliding a window of 32 RGB frames with a stride of 8 frames.

We chose not to crop out the face region of the video and keep the entire image as input to the network. Indeed, the video is already centered on the person and we expect that the movement of the body such as the hands can be a good indicator for the emotion recognition and sentiment analysis tasks.

5 Dataset

We test our joint-encoding solution on a novel dataset for multimodal sentiment and emotion recognition called CMU-Multimodal Opinion Sentiment and Emotion Intensity (CMU-MOSEI, Zadeh et al. (2018b)). It consists of 23,453 annotated sentences from 1000 distinct speakers. Each sentence is annotated for sentiment on a [-3,3] scale from highly negative (-3) to highly positive (+3) and for emotion by 6 classes : happiness, sadness, anger, fear, disgust, surprise. In the scope of our experiment, the emotions are

| Test set | Sentiment | | Emotions | | | | | | | | | | | |
| | 2-class | 7-class | Happy | | Sad | | Angry | | Fear | | Disgust | | Surprise | |
	A	A	A	F1	A	F1	A	F1	A	F1	A	F1	A	F1
L+ A + V	81.5	44.4	65.0	64.0	72.0	67.9	81.6	74.7	89.1	84.0	85.9	83.6	90.5	86.1
L + A	**82.4**	**45.5**	**66.0**	65.5	**73.9**	67.9	**81.9**	76.0	**89.2**	**87.2**	**86.5**	84.5	**90.6**	**86.1**
L	81.9	44.2	64.5	63.4	72.9	65.8	81.4	75.3	89.1	84.0	86.6	84.5	90.5	81.4
Mu-Net	82.1	-	-	**68.4**	-	**74.5**	-	**80.9**	-	87.0	-	**87.3**	-	80.9
G-MFN	76.9	45.0	-	66.3	-	66.9	-	72.8	-	89.9	-	76.6	-	85.5

Table 1: Results on the test-set. Note that the F1-scores for emotions are weighted to be consistent with the previous state-of-the-art. Also, we do not compare accuracies for emotions, as previous works use a weighted variant while we use standard accuracy. G-MFN is the Graph-MFN model and Mu-Net is the Multilogue-Net model.

either present or not present (binary classification), but two emotions can be present at the same time, making it a multi-label problem.

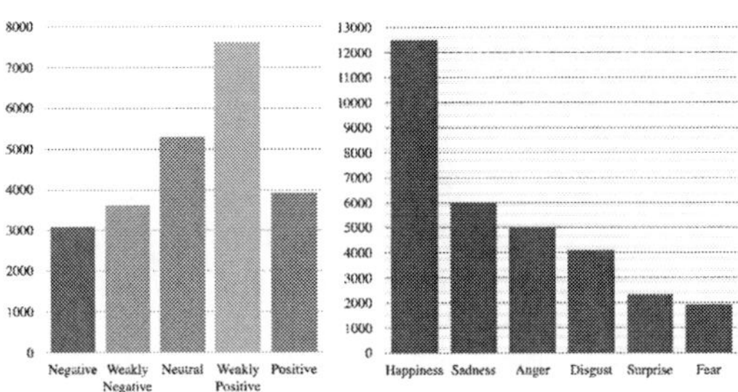

Figure 3: MOSEI statistics, taken from the author's paper.

The Figure 3 shows the distribution of sentiment and emotions in CMU-MOSEI dataset. The distribution shows a natural skew towards more frequently used emotions. The most common category is happiness with more than 12,000 positive sample points. The least prevalent emotion is fear with almost 1900 positive sample. It also shows a slight shift in favor of positive sentiment.

6 Experiments

In this section, we report the results of our model variants described in Section 3. We first explain our experimental setting.

6.1 Experimental settings

We train our models using the Adam optimizer (Kingma and Ba, 2014) with a learning rate of $1e - 4$ and a mini-batch size of 32. If the accuracy score on the validation set does not increase for a given epoch, we apply a learning-rate decay of factor 0.2. We decay our learning rate up to 2 times. Afterwards, we use an early-stop of 3 epochs. Results presented in this paper are from the averaged predictions of 5 models.

Unless stated otherwise, we use 6 Transformer blocks of hidden-size 512, regardless of the modality encoded. The self-attention has 4 multi-heads and the MLP has one hidden layer of 1024. We apply dropout of 0.1 on the output of each block (equation 4) and of 0.5 on the input of the classification layer (s in equation 6).

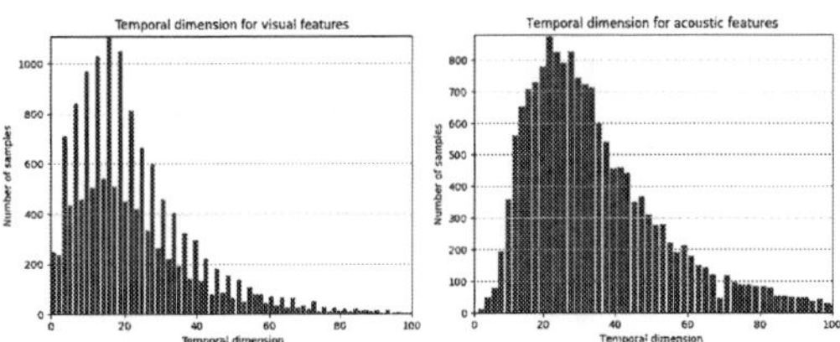

Figure 4: Temporal dimension (i.e. rows in our feature matrices) for the acoustic and visual modality.

For the acoustic and visual features, we truncate the features for spatial dimensions above 40. We also use that number for the number of glimpses. This choice is made base on Figure 4

6.2 Results

The Table 1 show the scores of our different modality combinations. We do not compare accuracies for emotions with previous works as they used a weighted accuracy variant while we use standard accuracy.

We notice that our L+A (linguistic + acoustic) is the best model. Unfortunately, adding the visual input did not increase the results, showing that it is still the most difficult modality to integrate into a multimodal pipeline. For the sentiment task, the improvement is more tangible for the 7-class, showing that our L+A model learns better representations for more complex classification problems compared to our monomodal model L using only the linguistic input. We also surpass the previous state-of-the-art for this task. For the emotions, we can see that Multilogue-Net gives better prediction for some classes, such as happy, sad, angry and disgust. We postulate that this is because Multilogue is a context-aware method while our model does not take into account the previous or next sentence to predict the current utterance. This might affect our accuracy and f1-score on the emotion task.

The following Table 2 depicts the results of our solution sent to the Second Grand-Challenge on Multimodal Language. It has been evaluated on the private test-fold released for the challenge and can serve as a baseline for future research. Note that in this table, the F1-scores are unweighted, as should be future results for a fair comparison and interpretation of the results.

Sentiment	7-class
L + A (A)	40.20

Emotion	Happy	Sad	Angry
L + A (A)	67.07	82.66	81.65
L + A (F1)	78.08	31.42	28.38

Emotion	Fear	Disgust	Surprise
L + A (A)	88.19	79.14	90.45
L + A (F1)	26.66	25.49	15.82

Table 2: Results on the private test-fold for 7-class sentiment problem and for each emotion. Accuracy is denoted by A. In this table, the F1-scores are unweighted, unlike Table 1.

7 Discussions

We presented a computationally efficient and robust model for Sentiment Analysis and Emotion Recognition evaluated on CMU-MOSEI. Though we showed strong results on accuracy, we can see that there is still a lot of room for improvement on the F1-scores, especially for the emotion classes that are less present in the dataset. To the best of our knowledge, the results presented by our transformer-based joint-encoding are the strongest scores for the sentiment task on the dataset.

The following list identifies other features we

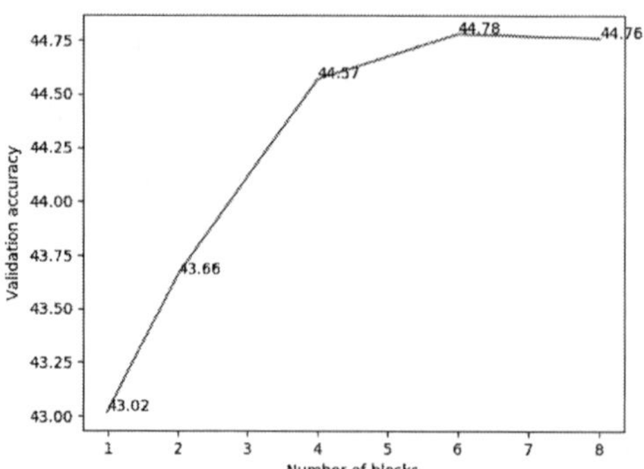

Figure 5: 7-class sentiment accuracy according to the number of blocks per Transformer.

computed as input for our model that lead to weaker performances:

- We tried the OpenFace 2.0 features (Baltrusaitis et al., 2018). This strategy computes facial landmark, the features are specialized for facial behavior analysis;

- We tried a simple 2D CNN named DenseNet (Huang et al., 2017). For each frame of the video, a feature vector is extracted by taking the output of the average pooling layer;

- We tried different values for the number of mel filter bank (512 and 1024) and temporal reduction (1, 2, 4 and 8 frames), we also tried to use the full spectrogram;

- We tried not using the GloVe embedding.

8 Acknowledgements

Noé Tits is funded through a FRIA grant (Fonds pour la Formation à la Recherche dans l'Industrie et l'Agriculture, Belgium).

References

Jimmy Lei Ba, Jamie Ryan Kiros, and Geoffrey E Hinton. 2016. Layer normalization. *arXiv preprint arXiv:1607.06450.*

Tadas Baltrusaitis, Amir Zadeh, Yao Chong Lim, and Louis-Philippe Morency. 2018. Openface 2.0: Facial behavior analysis toolkit. In *13th IEEE International Conference on Automatic Face & Gesture Recognition*, pages 59–66. IEEE.

Gao Huang, Zhuang Liu, Laurens Van Der Maaten, and Kilian Q Weinberger. 2017. Densely connected convolutional networks. In *Proceedings of the IEEE*

Conference on Computer Vision and Pattern Recognition, pages 4700–4708.

Diederik P Kingma and Jimmy Ba. 2014. Adam: A method for stochastic optimization. *arXiv preprint arXiv:1412.6980*.

Brian McFee, Colin Raffel, Dawen Liang, Daniel PW Ellis, Matt McVicar, Eric Battenberg, and Oriol Nieto. 2015. librosa: Audio and music signal analysis in python. In *Proceedings of the 14th python in science conference*, pages 18–25.

Jeffrey Pennington, Richard Socher, and Christopher D Manning. 2014. Glove: Global vectors for word representation. In *EMNLP*, volume 14, pages 1532–1543.

Saurav Sahay, Shachi H Kumar, Rui Xia, Jonathan Huang, and Lama Nachman. 2018. Multimodal relational tensor network for sentiment and emotion classification. In *Proceedings of Grand Challenge and Workshop on Human Multimodal Language (Challenge-HML)*, pages 20–27, Melbourne, Australia. Association for Computational Linguistics.

Aman Shenoy and Ashish Sardana. 2020. Multiloguenet: A context aware rnn for multi-modal emotion detection and sentiment analysis in conversation.

Hideyuki Tachibana, Katsuya Uenoyama, and Shunsuke Aihara. 2018. Efficiently trainable text-to-speech system based on deep convolutional networks with guided attention. In *2018 IEEE International Conference on Acoustics, Speech and Signal Processing (ICASSP)*, pages 4784–4788. IEEE.

Du Tran, Lubomir Bourdev, Rob Fergus, Lorenzo Torresani, and Manohar Paluri. 2015. Learning spatiotemporal features with 3d convolutional networks. In *Proceedings of the IEEE International Conference on Computer Vision*, pages 4489–4497.

Du Tran, Heng Wang, Lorenzo Torresani, Jamie Ray, Yann LeCun, and Manohar Paluri. 2018. A closer look at spatiotemporal convolutions for action recognition. In *Proceedings of the IEEE Conference on Computer Vision and Pattern Recognition (CVPR)*, pages 6450–6459.

Ashish Vaswani, Noam Shazeer, Niki Parmar, Jakob Uszkoreit, Llion Jones, Aidan N Gomez, Łukasz Kaiser, and Illia Polosukhin. 2017. Attention is all you need. In *Advances in neural information processing systems*, pages 5998–6008.

Zhou Yu, Jun Yu, Yuhao Cui, Dacheng Tao, and Qi Tian. 2019. Deep modular co-attention networks for visual question answering. In *Proceedings of the IEEE Conference on Computer Vision and Pattern Recognition*, pages 6281–6290.

Amir Zadeh, Paul Pu Liang, Navonil Mazumder, Soujanya Poria, Erik Cambria, and Louis-Philippe Morency. 2018a. Memory fusion network for multiview sequential learning. In *Thirty-Second AAAI Conference on Artificial Intelligence*.

AmirAli Zadeh, Paul Pu Liang, Soujanya Poria, Erik Cambria, and Louis-Philippe Morency. 2018b. Multimodal language analysis in the wild: CMU-MOSEI dataset and interpretable dynamic fusion graph. In *Proceedings of the 56th Annual Meeting of the Association for Computational Linguistics (Volume 1: Long Papers)*, pages 2236–2246, Melbourne, Australia. Association for Computational Linguistics.

A Multi-modal Approach to Fine-grained Opinion Mining on Video Reviews

Edison Marrese-Taylor[1*], Cristian Rodriguez-Opazo[2*], Jorge A. Balazs[1]
Stephen Gould[2] and Yutaka Matsuo[1]
Graduate School of Engineering, The University of Tokyo, Japan[1]
{emarrese, jorge, matsuo}@weblab.t.u-tokyo.ac.jp
Australian Centre for Robotic Vision (ACRV), Australian National University[2]
{cristian.rodriguez, stephen.gould}@anu.edu.au
*Authors contributed equally to this work.

Abstract

Despite the recent advances in opinion mining for written reviews, few works have tackled the problem on other sources of reviews. In light of this issue, we propose a multi-modal approach for mining fine-grained opinions from video reviews that is able to determine the aspects of the item under review that are being discussed and the sentiment orientation towards them. Our approach works at the sentence level without the need for time annotations and uses features derived from the audio, video and language transcriptions of its contents. We evaluate our approach on two datasets and show that leveraging the video and audio modalities consistently provides increased performance over text-only baselines, providing evidence these extra modalities are key in better understanding video reviews.

1 Introduction

Sentiment analysis (SA) is an important task in natural language processing, aiming at identifying and extracting opinions, emotions, and subjectivity. As a result, sentiment can be automatically collected, analyzed and summarized. Because of this, SA has received much attention not only in academia but also in industry, helping provide feedback based on customers' opinions about products or services. The underlying assumption in SA is that the entire input has an overall polarity, however, this is usually not the case. For example, laptop reviews generally not only express the overall sentiment about a specific model (e.g., "This is a great laptop"), but also relate to its specific aspects, such as the hardware, software or price. Subsequently, a review may convey opposing sentiments (e.g., "Its performance is ideal, I wish I could say the same about the price") or objective information (e.g., "This one still has the CD slot") for different aspects of an entity. Aspect-based sentiment analysis (ABSA) or fine-grained opinion mining aims to extract opinion targets or aspects of entities being reviewed in a text, and to determine the sentiment reviewers express for each. ABSA allows us to evaluate aggregated sentiments for each aspect of a given product or service and gain a more granular understanding of their quality. This is of especial interest for companies as it enables them to refine specifications for a given product or service, and leading to an improved overall customer satisfaction.

Fine-grained opinion mining is also important for a variety of NLP tasks, including opinion-oriented question answering and opinion summarization. In practical terms, the ABSA task can be divided into two sub-steps, namely aspect extraction (*AE*) and (aspect level) sentiment classification (*SC*), which can be tackled in a pipeline fashion, or simultaneously (*AESC*). These tasks can be regarded as a token-level sequence labeling problem, and are generally tackled using supervised learning. The 2014 and 2015 SemEval workshops, co-located with COLING 2014 and NAACL 2015 respectively, included shared tasks on ABSA (Pontiki et al., 2014) and also followed this approach, which has also served as a way to encourage developments alongside this line of research (Mitchell et al., 2013; Irsoy and Cardie, 2014; Liu et al., 2015; Zhang et al., 2015).

The flexibility provided by the deep learning setting has helped multi-modal approaches to bloom. Examples of this include tasks such as machine translation (Specia et al., 2016; Elliott et al., 2017), word sense disambiguation (Chen et al., 2015), visual question answering (Chen et al., 2017), language grounding (Beinborn et al.; Lazaridou et al., 2015), and sentiment analysis (Poria et al., 2015; Zadeh et al., 2016). Specifically in this last example, the task focuses on generalizing text-based sentiment analysis to opinionated videos, where three communicative modalities are present: language (spoken words), visual (gestures), and acoustic (voice).

Although reviews often come under the form of a written commentary, people are increasingly turning to video platforms such as YouTube looking for product reviews to help them shop. In this context, Marrese-Taylor et al. (2017) explored a new direction, arguing that video reviews are the natural evolution of written product reviews and introduced a dataset of annotated video product review transcripts. Similarly, Garcia et al. (2019b) recently presented an improved version of the POM movie review dataset (Park et al., 2014),

Proceedings of the 58th Annual Meeting of the Association for Computational Linguistics, pages 8–18
Seattle, USA, July5 - 10, 2020. ©2017 Association for Computational Linguistics
https://doi.org/10.18653/v1/P17

with annotated fine-grained opinions.

Although the videos in these kinds of datasets represent a rich multi-modal source of opinions, the features of the language in them may fundamentally differ from written reviews given that information is conveyed through multiple channels (one for speech, one for gestures, one for facial expressions, one for vocal inflections, etc.) In these, different information channels complement each other to maximize the coherence and clarity of their message. This means that although the content of each channel may be comprehended in isolation, in theory we need to process the information in all the channels simultaneously to fully comprehend the message (Hasan et al., 2019). In this context, information extracted from nonverbal language in videos, such as gestures and facial expressions, as well as from audio in the manner of voice inflections or pauses, and from scenes, object or images in the video, become critical for performing well.

In light of this, our paper introduces a multi-modal approach for fine-grained opinion mining. We conduct extensive experiments on two datasets built upon transcriptions of video reviews, Youtubean (Marrese-Taylor et al., 2017) and a fine-grain annotated version of the Persuasive Opinion Multimedia (POM) dataset (Park et al., 2014; Garcia et al., 2019b), adapting them to our setting by associating timestamps to each annotated sentence using the video subtitles. Our results demonstrate the effectiveness of our proposed approach and show that by leveraging the additional modalities we can consistently obtain better performance.

2   Related Work

Our work is related to aspect extraction using deep learning, a task that is often tackled as a sequence labeling problem. In particular, our work is related to Irsoy and Cardie (2014), who pioneered in the field by using multi-layered RNNs. Later, Liu et al. (2015) successfully adapted the architectures by Mesnil et al. (2013) which were originally developed for slot-filling in the context of Natural Language Understanding.

Literature offers related work on the usage of RNNs for open domain targeted sentiment (Mitchell et al., 2013), where Zhang et al. (2015) experimented with neural CRF models using various RNN architectures on a dataset of informal language from Twitter.

Regarding target-based sentiment analysis, the literature contains several ad-hoc models that account for the sentence structure and the position of the aspect on it (Tang et al., 2016a,b). These approaches mainly use attention-augmented RNNs for solving the task. However, they require the location of the aspect to be known in advance and therefore are only useful in pipeline models, while instead we model aspect extraction and sentiment classification as a joint task or using multi-tasking.

AESC has also often been tackled as a sequence labeling problem, mainly using Conditional Random Fields (CRFs) (Mitchell et al., 2013). To model the problem in this fashion, collapsed or sentiment-bearing IOB labels (Zhang et al., 2015) are used. Pipeline models (i.e. task-independent model ensembles) have also been extensively studied by the same authors. Xu et al. (2014) performed *AESC* by modeling the linking relation between aspects and the sentiment-bearing phrases.

When it comes to the video review domain, there is related work on YouTube mining, mainly focused on exploiting user comments. For example, Wu et al. (2014) exploited crowdsourced textual data from time-synced commented videos, proposing a temporal topic model based on LDA. Tahara et al. (2010) introduced a similar approach for *Nico Nico*, using time-indexed social annotations to search for desirable scenes inside videos.

On the other hand, Severyn et al. (2014) proposed a systematic approach to mine user comments that relies on tree kernel models. Additionally, Krishna et al. (2013) performed sentiment analysis on YouTube comments related to popular topics using machine learning techniques, showing that the trends in users' sentiments is well correlated to the corresponding real-world events. Siersdorfer et al. (2010) presented an analysis of dependencies between comments and comment ratings, proving that community feedback in combination with term features in comments can be used for automatically determining the community acceptance of comments.

We also find some papers that have successfully attempted to use closed caption mining for video activity recognition (Gupta and Mooney, 2010) and scene segmentation (Gupta and Mooney, 2009). Similar work has been done using closed captions to classify movies by genre (Brezeale and Cook, 2006) and summarize video programs (Brezeale and Cook, 2006). Regarding multi-modal approaches for sentiment analysis, we see that previous work has focused mainly on sentiment classification, or the related task of emotion detection (Lakomkin et al., 2017), where the CMU MOSI dataset (Zadeh et al., 2016) appears as the main resource. In this setting, the main problem is how to model and capture cross-modality interactions to predict the sentiment correctly. In this regard Zadeh et al. (2017) proposed a tensor fusion layer that can better capture cross-modality interactions between text, audio and video inputs, while Poria et al. (2017) modeled inter-dependencies across difference utterances of a single video, obtaining further improvements.

Blanchard et al. (2018) are, to the best of our knowledge, the first to tackle scalable multi-modal sentiment classification using both visual and acoustic modalities. More recently Ghosal et al. (2018) proposed an RNN-based multi-modal approach that relies on attention to learn the contributing features among multi-utterance representations. On the other hand Pham et al. (2018) introduced multi-modal sequence-to-sequence models which perform specially well in bi-modal settings. Finally, Akhtar et al. (2019) proposed a multi-modal, multi-task approach in which the inputs from a video (text, acoustic and visual frames), are exploited for simultaneously predicting the sentiment and expressed emotions of an utterance. Our work is related to all of these approaches, but it is different in that we apply multi-modal techniques not only for sentiment classification, but also for aspect extraction.

Finally, Marrese-Taylor et al. (2017) and Garcia et al. (2019b) contributed multi-modal datasets obtained from product and movie reviews respectively, specifically for the task of fine-grained opinion mining. Furthermore, Garcia et al. (2019a) recently used the latter to propose a hierarchical multi-modal model for opinion mining. Compared to them, our approach follows a more traditional setting for fine-grained opinion mining, while also offering a more general framework for the problem. Garcia et al. (2019a) utilize a single encoder that receives as input the concatenation of the features for each modality, for each token. This requires explicit alignment between the features of the different modalities at the token level. In contrast, since each modality is encoded separately in our approach, we only require the feature alignment to be at the sentence level.

3 Task Description

Opinion mining can be performed at several levels of granularity, the most common ones being the sentence level, and the more fine-grained aspect level. Fine-grained opinion mining can be further subdivided in two tasks: aspect extraction and aspect-level sentiment classification. The former deals with finding the aspects being referred to, and the latter with associating them with a sentiment.

Previous work usually casts this task as a sequence-labeling problem, where models have to predict whether a token is a part of an aspect and infer its sentiment polarity (Mitchell et al., 2013; Zhang et al., 2015; Liu et al., 2015). Depending on the dataset annotations, aspect categories are in some cases specified as well.

Formally, given a sentence $s = [x_1, \ldots, x_n]$, we want to automatically annotate each token x_i with its aspect membership and polarity. In the simpler case where we only want to perform Aspect Extraction, a common annotation scheme is to tag each token with a label $y_i \in \mathbb{L}^{AE}$ where $\mathbb{L}^{AE} = \{I, O, B\}$. In this scheme, commonly known as IOB, O labels indicate that a token is not a member of an aspect, B labels indicate that a token is at the beginning of an aspect, and I labels indicate that the token is inside an aspect.

Similarly, performing token-level Sentiment Classification only is equivalent to tagging each token with a label $y_i \in \mathbb{L}^{SC}$ where $\mathbb{L}^{SC} = \{\phi, +, -\}$, and ϕ denotes no sentiment, $+$ denotes a positive polarity and $-$ a negative one.

It is also possible to define a *collapsed* annotation scheme, where aspect membership and sentiment polarity are encoded in a single tag. We define the label set for this setting as $\mathbb{L}^{C} = \{O, B+, B-, I+, I-\}$.

Table 1 shows the possible ways to annotate the sentence "I love the saturated colors!" under these three annotation schemes, where the aspect being referred to is "saturated colors".

	I	love	the	saturated	colors	!
$\mathbb{L}^{AE}$	O	O	O	B	I	O
$\mathbb{L}^{SC}$	ϕ	ϕ	ϕ	$+$	$+$	ϕ
$\mathbb{L}^{C}$	O	O	O	$B+$	$I+$	O

Table 1: Label definition alternatives for the tasks in ABSA using sequence labeling.

Labels can be further augmented with type information. For example Liu et al. (2015) used different tags for opinion targets (e.g. B-TARG), and opinion expressions (e.g., B-EXPR), however, we do not rely on this information.

4 Proposed Approach

We propose a multi-modal approach for aspect extraction and sentiment classification that leverages video, audio and textual features. This approach assumes we have a video review v containing opinions, its extracted audio stream a, and a transcription of the audio into a sequence of sentences $\mathbb{S}$. Further, each sentence $s \in \mathbb{S}$ is annotated with its respective start and end times in the video effectively mapping them to a video segment $v^s \subset v$ and its corresponding audio segment $a^s \subset a$. These segments do not necessarily cover the whole video i.e. $\cup v^s \subset v$ since the reviews may include parts that have no speech and therefore no sentences are associated to those. Our end goal is to produce a sequence of labels $l = [y_1, \ldots, y_n]$ for each sentence $s = [x_1, \ldots, x_n]$ while exploiting the information contained in v^s and a^s.

Figure 1 presents a high-level overview of our approach. We rely on an encoder-decoder paradigm to create separate representations for each modality (Cho et al., 2014). The text encoding module generates a representation for each token in the input text, while the video and audio encoding layers produce utterance-level representations from each modality.

We propose combining these representations with an approach inspired by early-fusion (Xu et al., 2018), which allows for the word-level representations to interact with audio and visual features. Finally, a sequence labeling module is in charge of taking the final token-level representations and producing a token-level label. In the following sub-sections we describe each component of our model.

4.1 Text Encoding Module

This module generates a representation of the natural language input so that the obtained representation is

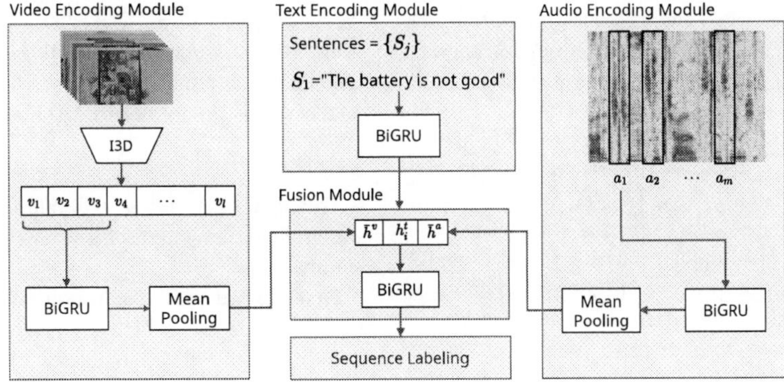

Figure 1: Overview of our proposed approach for multi-modal opinion mining

useful for the sequence labeling task. Our text encoder first maps each word x_i into an embedded input sequence $x = [x_1, \ldots, x_n]$, then projects this into a vector $h_i^t \in \mathbb{R}^{d_t}$, where d_t corresponds to the hidden dimension of the obtained text representation. Although our text encoding module is generic, in this paper we implement it as a bi-directional GRU (Cho et al., 2014), on top of pre-trained word embeddings, specifically GloVe (Pennington et al., 2014), as follows.

$$h_i^t = \text{BiGRU}(x_i, h_{i-1}^t) \tag{1}$$

4.2 Audio Encoding Module

We assume the existence of a finite set of time-ordered audio features $a = [a_1, \ldots, a_m]$ extracted from each audio utterance a^s, for instance with the procedure described in Section 5.2. We feed these vectors into another bi-directional GRU to add context to each time step, obtaining hidden states $h_j^a \in \mathbb{R}^{d_a}$.

$$h_j^a = \text{BiGRU}(a_j, h_{j-1}^a) \tag{2}$$

To obtain a condensed representation from the audio signal we again utilize mean pooling over the intermediate memory vectors, obtaining $\bar{h}^a$.

4.3 Video Encoding Module

We propose a video encoding layer that generates a visual representation summarizing spatio-temporal patterns directly from the raw input frames. Concretely, given a video segment $v = [v_1, \ldots, v_T]$, where v_i is a vector representing a single frame in v^s, our encoding module first maps this sequence into another sequence of video features $\hat{v} = [\hat{v}_1, \ldots, \hat{v}_l]$ following the method described in Section 5.2. Later, this new sequence is mapped into a vector $\bar{h}^v \in \mathbb{R}^{d_v}$ that captures summarized high-level visual semantics in the video, as follows:

$$h_k^v = \text{BiGRU}(\hat{v}_k, h_{k-1}^v) \tag{3}$$

4.4 Fusion Module

We utilize an early fusion strategy similar to Xu et al. (2018) to aggregate the representations obtained from each modality. We concatenate the contextualized representation h_i^t for each token to the summarized representations of the additional modalities, $\bar{h}^a$ and $\bar{h}^v$, and feed this final vector representation to an additional BiGRU:

$$h_i = \text{BiGRU}([h_i^t; \bar{h}^a; \bar{h}^v], h_{i-1}) \tag{4}$$

As a result, our model now allows the representation of each word in the input sentence to interact with the audio and visual features, enabling it to learn potentially different ways to associate each word with the additional modalities. An alternative way to achieve this would be to utilize attention mechanisms to enforce such association behavior, however, we instead let the model learn this relation without using any additional inductive bias.

4.5 Sequence Labeling Module

The main labeling module is a multi-layer perceptron guided by a self attention component. The self attention component enriches the representation h_i with contextual information coming from every other sequence element by performing the following operations:

$$u_{i,j} = v_\alpha^\top \tanh(W_\alpha[h_i; h_j] + b_\alpha) \tag{5}$$

$$\alpha_{i,j} = \text{softmax}(u_{i,j}) \tag{6}$$

$$t_i = \sum_{j=1}^{n} \alpha_{i,j} \cdot h_j \tag{7}$$

$$o_i = W_l[h_i; t_i] + b_l \tag{8}$$

Where o_i is a vector associated to input x_i, and v_α, W_α, W_l and b_α, b_l are trainable parameters. As shown, these vectors are obtained using both the corresponding *aligned* input h_i and the attention-weighted vector t_i.

Following previous work, we feed these vectors into a Linear Chain CRF layer, which performs the final labeling. Neural CRFs have proven to be especially effective for various sequence segmentation or labeling tasks in NLP (Ma and Hovy, 2016; Yang and Zhang,

2018; Yang et al., 2018), and have also been used successfully in the past for open domain opinion mining (Zhang et al., 2015). Concretely, we model emission and transition potentials as follows.

$$\psi_i := e(x_i, y_i; \theta) = \boldsymbol{h}_i \cdot \boldsymbol{y}_i \qquad (9)$$

$$\psi_{i,j} := q(y_i, y_j; \boldsymbol{\Pi}) = \boldsymbol{\Pi}_{y_i, y_j} \qquad (10)$$

Where $\boldsymbol{h}_i$ is the fused hidden state for position i and θ denotes the parameters involved in computing this vector, $\boldsymbol{y}_i$ is a one-hot vector associated to y_i, and $\boldsymbol{\Pi}$ is a trainable matrix of size $\mathbb{L}^{AE}$ or $\mathbb{L}^C$ depending on the setting —see Section 5 for more details on this. The score function of a given input sentence s and output sequence of labels l is defined as:

$$\Phi(s, l) = \sum_{i=1}^{n} \log e(x, y_i; \theta) + \log q(y_i, y_{i-1}; \boldsymbol{\Pi}) \quad (11)$$

In this work we directly optimize the negative log-likelihood associated to this score during training, and apply Viterbi decoding during inference to obtain the most likely labels.

5 Experimental Setup

We evaluate our proposal in several experimental settings based on previous work.

- **Simple**: We only focus on the task of aspect extraction, following a sequence labeling approach with regular IOB tags in $\mathbb{L}^{AE}$.

- **Collapsed Aspect-Level (CAL)**: We perform aspect extraction and aspect-level sentiment classification with a sequence labeling model, utilizing sentiment-bearing IOB tags in $\mathbb{L}^C$.

- **Collapsed Sentence-Level (CSL)**: Like the previous setting, but we only keep sentence examples that contain a single sentiment, so we can perform sentence-level sentiment classification. Again, we use sequence labeling with sentiment-bearing IOB tags in $\mathbb{L}^C$.

- **Joint Sentence-Level (JSL)**: We use a multi-tasking approach and perform sequence labeling for aspect extraction with regular IOB tags in $\mathbb{L}^{AE}$, and sequence classification to predict the sentence-level sentiment. In this sense, we add a final 3-layer fully-connected neural network that receives a mean-pooled representation of the fusion layer $\bar{h} = \frac{1}{n} \sum_{i=1}^{n} \boldsymbol{h}_i$ and predicts a sentence-level sentiment. As loss function we utilize the mini-batch average cross-entropy with the gold standard class label. The total loss is the sum of the losses for sequence labeling and sequence classification.

Previous work has also shown that most sentences present a single aspect, and therefore a single sentiment

(Marrese-Taylor et al., 2017; Zuo et al., 2018; Zhao et al., 2010), which motivates the introduction of the CSL and JSL settings. For these cases we filtered out sentences that do not fit this description.

5.1 Data

We report results on two different datasets containing fine-grained annotations for both opinion targets and sentiment.

First, we work with the Youtubean dataset (Marrese-Taylor et al., 2017), which contains sentences extracted from YouTube video annotated with aspects and their respective sentiments. The data comes from the user-provided closed-captions derived from 7 different long product review videos about a cell phone, totaling up to 71 minutes of audiovisual data. In total there are 578 long sentences from free spoken descriptions of the product, on average each sentence consist of 20 words. The dataset has a total of 525 aspects, with more than 66% of the sentences containing at least one mention.

Second, we work with the fine-grained annotations gathered for the POM dataset by Garcia et al. (2019b). This dataset is composed of 1000 videos containing reviews where a single speaker in frontal view makes a critique of a movie that he/she has watched. There are videos from 372 unique speakers, with 600 different movie titles being reviewed. Each video has an average length of about 94 seconds and contains 15.1 sentences on average. The fine-grained annotations we utilize are available for each token indicating if it is responsible for the understanding of the polarity of the sentence, and whether it describes the target of an opinion; each sentence has an average of 22.5 tokens. We assume that whenever there is an overlap between the span annotations for a given target and a certain polarity, the corresponding polarity can be assigned to that target, otherwise it is labeled as neutral.

Since the annotated sentences in both datasets are not associated to specific timestamps, in this work we propose a method based on heuristics to rescue the video segments that correspond to each annotated sentence by leveraging video subtitles (or closed-captions.)

```
168
00:20:41,150 —> 00:20:45,109
- How did he do that?
- Made him an offer he could not refuse.
```

Figure 2: Excerpt of a subtitle chunk (in SubRip format,) showing its main components.

As shown in Figure 2, closed captions or subtitles are composed of chunks that contain: (1) A numeric counter identifying each chunk, (2) The time at which the subtitle should appear on the screen followed by `-->` and the time when it should disappear, (3) The subtitle text itself on one or more lines, and (4) A blank line containing no text, indicating the end of this subtitle. These chunks exhibit a large variance in terms of their length, meaning that sentences are usually split into many chunks.

Starting from a subtitle file associated to a given product review video, we apply a fuzzy-matching approach between each annotated sentence for that review and each closed caption chunk. This is repeated for each one of the videos in our datasets. Whenever an annotated sentence matches exactly or has over 90% similarity with a closed caption chunk, its time-span is associated to that sentence. Finally, the "start" and "end" timestamps assigned to each sentence are defined by the start and end time spans of their first and last associated closed captions, sorted by time.

5.2 Implementation Details

Pre-processing for the natural language input is performed utilizing spacy[1], which we use mainly to tokenize. Input sentences are trimmed to a maximum length of 300 tokens, and tokens with frequency lower than 1 are replaced with a special *UNK* marker. To work with the POM dataset, which is already tokenized, we first convert it to the ABSA format, which is tokenization agnostic, and then we process it.

Although our audio encoder is generic, in this work we follow Lakomkin et al. (2017) and use Fast Fourier Transform spectrograms to extract rich vectors from each audio segment. Specifically, we use a window length of 1024 points and 512 points overlap, giving us vectors of size 513. Alternative audio feature extractors such as Degottex et al. (2014) could also be utilized.

On the other hand, in this work we model video feature extraction using I3D (Carreira and Zisserman, 2017). This method inflates the 2D filters of a well-known network e.g. Inception (Szegedy et al., 2015; Ioffe and Szegedy, 2015) or ResNet (He et al., 2016) for image classification to obtain 3D filters, helping us better exploit the spatio-temporal nature of video. We first pre-process the videos by extracting features of size 1024 using I3D with average pooling, taking as input the raw frames of dimension 256×256, at 25 fps. We use the model pre-trained on the kinetics400 dataset (Kay et al., 2017) released by the same authors. Despite our choice to obtain video features, again we note that our video encoder is generic, so other alternatives such as C3D (Tran et al., 2015) could be utilized.

Finally, all of our models are trained in an end-to-end fashion using Adam (Kingma and Ba, 2014) with a learning rate of 10^{-3}. To prevent over-fitting, we add dropout to the text encoding layer. We use a batch size of 8 for the Youtubean dataset, and of 64 for the POM dataset. The language encoder uses a hidden state of size 150, and we fine-tune the pre-trained GloVe.

On each case we compare the performance of our proposed approach against a baseline model that does not consider multi-modality, does not utilize pre-trained GloVe word embeddings and is based on a cross-entropy loss, in which case we simply utilize

the mini-batch average cross-entropy between $\hat{y}_i =$ softmax(o_i) and the gold standard one-hot encoded labels y_i, a vector that is the size of the tag label vocabulary for the corresponding task.

5.3 Evaluation

Since the size of Youtubean is relatively small, all our experiments in this dataset are evaluated using 5-fold cross validation. In the case of the POM dataset, we report performance on the validation and test sets averaging results for 5 different random seeds. In both cases we compare models using paired two-sided t-tests to check for statistical significance of the differences.

To evaluate our sequence labeling tasks we used the CoNLL *conlleval* script, taking the aspect extraction F1-score as our model selection metric for early stopping. To perform joint aspect extraction and sentiment classification, we considered *positive*, *negative* and *neutral* as sentiment classes, and decoupled the IOB collapsed tags using simple heuristics. Concretely, we recover the aspect extraction F1-score as well as classification performances for each sentiment class.

6 Results

To evaluate the effectiveness of our proposals, we perform several ablation studies on the *Simple* setting for the Youtubean dataset. Using variations of our baseline with pre-trained GLoVe embeddings (GV), conditional random field (CRF), audio and video modalities (A+V). Experiments are also performed using 5-fold cross-validation, and comparisons are always tested for significance using paired two-sided t-tests.

As Table 4 shows, although every proposed model variation performs better than the baseline, only the model uses video and audio modalities obtains a statistically superior performance. We also see that our proposed multi-modal variation is the one that obtains the best performance, also being statistically significant at the highest level of confidence. We believe these results show that our proposed multi-modal architecture is not only able to exploit the features in the audio and video inputs, but it can also leverage the information in the pre-trained word embeddings and benefit from having an inductive bias that is tailored for the task at hand, in this case, with a loss based on structured prediction for sequence labeling.

Table 2 summarizes our results for the Youtubean dataset, where we can see that our proposed multi-modal approach is able to outperform the baseline model for all settings in the aspect extraction task. When it comes to sentiment classification, our multi-modal approaches do not obtain significant performance gain in all cases, sometimes performing worse although without statistical significance. We also compare our results to the performance reported by Marrese-Taylor et al. (2017), who experimented on the *Simple* and *CSL* settings. Their models also use pre-trained word embedding —although different from

---

[1] https://spacy.io

Setting	Model	Aspect Extraction			Sentiment Classification		
		P	R	F1	P	R	F1
Simple	Baseline	0.531	0.542	0.533	-	-	-
	Ours	**0.602****	**0.568**	**0.584*****	-	-	-
CAL	Baseline	0.546	0.538	0.539	0.710	0.688	0.696
	Ours	**0.590**	**0.572**	**0.581***	**0.722**	**0.722**	**0.718**
CSL	Baseline	0.526	0.463	0.490	**0.746**	**0.722**	**0.724**
	Ours	**0.563**	**0.581*****	**0.568****	0.720	0.674	0.688
JSL	Baseline	0.483	0.521	0.496	**0.946**	**0.946**	**0.946**
	Ours	**0.544*****	**0.552**	**0.545*****	**0.946**	**0.946**	**0.946**

Table 2: Summary of our results on the Youtubean dataset, *** denotes statistical significance at 99% confidence, ** at 95% and * at 90%.

Setting	Model	Aspect Extraction			Sentiment Classification		
		P	R	F1	P	R	F1
Simple	Baseline	0.394	0.379	0.386	-	-	-
	Ours	**0.396**	**0.406**	**0.399**	-	-	-
CAL	Baseline	0.364	**0.401***	0.382	**0.540*****	0.416	0.270
	Ours	**0.444****	0.368	**0.402****	0.488	**0.466*****	**0.342*****
CSL	Baseline	0.387	0.375	**0.408***	**0.614**	**0.446**	0.296
	Ours	**0.438***	**0.378**	0.404	0.532	**0.446**	**0.304**
JSL	Baseline	0.381	0.357	0.367	0.798	0.802	0.788
	Ours	**0.442*****	**0.401***	**0.420***	**0.924*****	**0.924*****	**0.922*****

Table 3: Summary of our results for the test set of the POM dataset, *** denotes statistical significance at 99% confidence, ** at 95% and * at 90%.

Model	Aspect Extraction		
	P	R	F1
T	0.532	0.543	0.533
T + CRF	0.558	0.528	0.541
T + GV	0.562	0.537	0.548
T + GV + CRF	0.576*	0.569	0.571**
T + A + V	0.587*	0.578	0.580*
T + CRF + A + V	0.578	0.570	0.573*
T + GV + CRF + A + V	0.602**	0.568	0.584***

Table 4: Ablation study on aspect extraction on the simple setting. *** denotes differences against the only text model (T) results are statistically significant at 99% confidence, ** at 95% and * at 90%. (A + V) refers to the audio and video modalities, (GV) stands for GLoVe embeddings and (CRF) for the model trained using the Conditional Random Fields loss.

Setting	Model	AE F1	SC F1
Simple	Baseline	0.428	-
	Ours	**0.433**	-
CAL	Baseline	0.412	0.240
	Ours	**0.427*****	**0.310****
CSL	Baseline	0.408	**0.264**
	Ours	**0.423***	0.262
JSL	Baseline	0.387	**0.950*****
	Ours	**0.469****	0.840

Table 5: Results for the validation set of the POM dataset, where *** denotes results are statistically significant at 99% confidence, ** at 95% and * at 90%.

GloVe— and as input they additionally receives binary features derived from POS tags and other word-level cues. We note, however, that they only experimented with a maximum length of 200 tokens, which makes our results not directly comparable. Their performance on aspect extraction for the *Simple* and *CAL* tasks are 0.561 and 0.555 F1-Score respectively, both of which are lower than ours. In terms of sentiment classification, they report results for each sentiment class with F1-Scores of 0.523, 0.149 and 0.811 for the positive,

negative and neutral classes, respectively. Our model is able to outperform this baseline, with a cross-class average F1-Score of 0.718. We do not deepen the analysis in this regard, as numbers are difficult to interpret without statistical testing.

Table 5 and Table 3 summarize our results for the *POM* dataset for the validation and test splits respectively. Compared to the previous dataset we see similar results where our multi-modal approach consistently outperforms the baseline for aspect extraction, but with the gains being comparatively smaller. We also see that our model is able to significantly outperform the baseline in the sentiment classification tasks at least in two

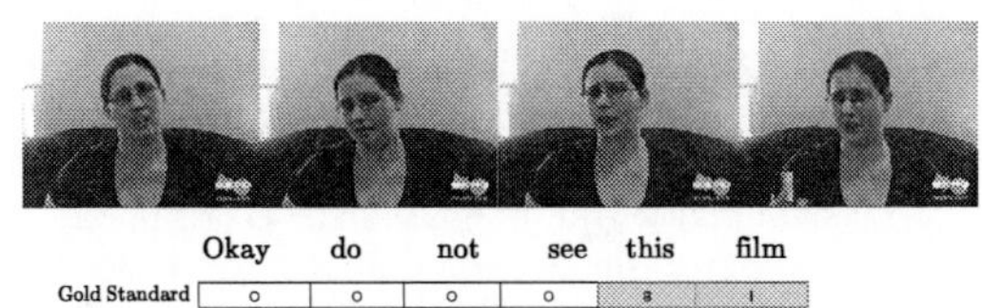

Figure 3: Qualitative comparison between baseline and our method on the POM dataset. Green and red boxes represent positive and negative sentiment respectively.

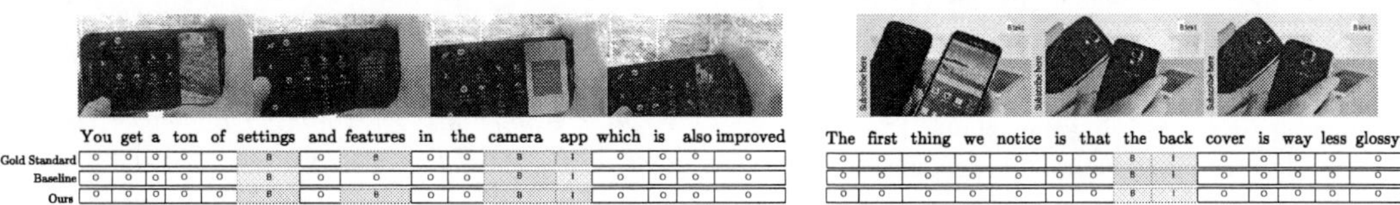

Figure 4: Qualitative comparison between baseline and our method on the Youtubean dataset. Green and yellow boxes represent positive and neutral sentiment respectively.

of out the three settings. In terms of previous work, our results cannot be directly compared to Garcia et al. (2019a) and Garcia et al. (2019b) as their problem setting is different from ours.

On a more broad perspective, we think the performance differences across datasets are related to the nature of each dataset. Meanwhile Youtubean contains reviews about actual physical products, which are often shown in the videos at the same time the reviewer is speaking, the POM dataset contains movie reviews where the speakers directly face the camera during most of the video, without utilizing any additional support material. As a result, the video reviews in the Youtubean dataset mainly focus on capturing images of the products under discussion, with relatively fewer scenes showing the reviewer. This means that there may be few visual cues in the manner of facial expressions or other specific actions that the models could exploit in order to perform better at the sentiment classification task, but more cues useful for aspect extraction. This situation is reverted in the POM dataset, which could explain why our models tend to perform better for sentiment classification, but offering smaller gains for the AE task.

We also think performance differences across datasets are to some extent explained by the nature of the annotations on each case. The annotation guidelines utilized to elaborate each dataset are actually quite different, with the annotations in the Youtubean dataset closely following those of the well-known SemEval datasets, which are target-centric and the POM standards substantially diverging from this. Concretely, Garcia et al. (2019b) propose a two-level annotation method, where "the smallest span of words that contains all the words necessary for the recognition of an opinion" are to be annotated. As a result, aspects annotated in the POM dataset often include pronouns which are more difficult to identify as aspects, often requiring co-reference resolution. With regards to aspect polarity, while it can be extracted directly from the Youtubean annotations, in the case of POM we needed some pre-processing as target and sentiment are annotated using independent text spans.

Qualitative results of the POM and Youtubean dataset in a multitask CAL can be seen in Figure 3 and 4 respectively, results suggest that the method learn to use the information from additional modalities and enhance the sentiment and aspect prediction.

Finally, as we observe that our models tend to obtain bigger gains on the AE tasks rather than on SC, we think this behavior can be partially attributed to the inductive bias of our model, which makes it specially suitable for sequence segmentation tasks.

7 Conclusions

In this paper we have presented a multi-modal approach for fine-grained opinion mining, introducing a modular architecture that utilizes features derived from the audio, video frames and language transcription of video reviews to perform aspect extraction and sentiment classification at the sentence level. To test our proposals we have taken two datasets built upon video review transcriptions containing fine-grained opinions, and introduced a technique that leverages the video subtitles to associate timestamps to each annotated sentence. Our results offer empirical evidence showing that the additional modalities contain useful information that can be exploited by our models to offer increased performance for both aspect extraction and sentiment classification, consistently outperforming text-only baselines.

For future work, we are interested in exploring other ways to capture cross-modal interactions, exploit the temporal relationship between the representations of different modalities, and test alternative ways to better deal with our multi-task settings.

Acknowledgments

We are grateful for the support provided by the NVIDIA Corporation, donating two of the GPUs used for this research.

References

Md Shad Akhtar, Dushyant Chauhan, Deepanway Ghosal, Soujanya Poria, Asif Ekbal, and Pushpak Bhattacharyya. 2019. Multi-task Learning for Multimodal Emotion Recognition and Sentiment Analysis. In *Proceedings of the 2019 Conference of the North*, pages 370–379, Minneapolis, Minnesota. Association for Computational Linguistics.

Lisa Beinborn, Teresa Botschen, and Iryna Gurevych. Multimodal Grounding for Language Processing. page 15.

Nathaniel Blanchard, Daniel Moreira, Aparna Bharati, and Walter Scheirer. 2018. Getting the subtext without the text: Scalable multimodal sentiment classification from visual and acoustic modalities. In *Proceedings of Grand Challenge and Workshop on Human Multimodal Language (Challenge-HML)*, pages 1–10, Melbourne, Australia. Association for Computational Linguistics.

Darin Brezeale and Diane Cook. 2006. Using closed captions and visual features to classify movies by genre. In *Proceedings of the 7th International Workshop on Multimedia Data Mining (MDM/KDD06): Poster Session*, Washington, DC, USA. ACM.

Joao Carreira and Andrew Zisserman. 2017. Quo vadis, action recognition? a new model and the kinetics dataset. In *CVPR*.

Danqi Chen, Adam Fisch, Jason Weston, and Antoine Bordes. 2017. Reading Wikipedia to Answer Open-Domain Questions. pages 1870–1879.

Xinlei Chen, Alan Ritter, Abhinav Gupta, and Tom Mitchell. 2015. Sense Discovery via Co-Clustering on Images and Text. pages 5298–5306.

Kyunghyun Cho, Bart van Merrienboer, Caglar Gulcehre, Dzmitry Bahdanau, Fethi Bougares, Holger Schwenk, and Yoshua Bengio. 2014. Learning Phrase Representations using RNN EncoderDecoder for Statistical Machine Translation. In *Proceedings of the 2014 Conference on Empirical Methods in Natural Language Processing (EMNLP)*, pages 1724–1734, Doha, Qatar. Association for Computational Linguistics.

Gilles Degottex, John Kane, Thomas Drugman, Tuomo Raitio, and Stefan Scherer. 2014. Covarepa collaborative voice analysis repository for speech technologies. In *2014 ieee international conference on acoustics, speech and signal processing (icassp)*, pages 960–964. IEEE.

Desmond Elliott, Stella Frank, Loc Barrault, Fethi Bougares, and Lucia Specia. 2017. Findings of the Second Shared Task on Multimodal Machine Translation and Multilingual Image Description. In *Proceedings of the Second Conference on Machine Translation*, pages 215–233, Copenhagen, Denmark. Association for Computational Linguistics.

Alexandre Garcia, Pierre Colombo, Florence d'Alché-Buc, Slim Essid, and Chloé Clavel. 2019a. From the Token to the Review: A Hierarchical Multimodal approach to Opinion Mining. In *Proceedings of the 2019 Conference on Empirical Methods in Natural Language Processing and the 9th International Joint Conference on Natural Language Processing (EMNLP-IJCNLP)*, pages 5542–5551, Hong Kong, China. Association for Computational Linguistics.

Alexandre Garcia, Slim Essid, Florence d'Alch Buc, and Chlo Clavel. 2019b. A multimodal movie review corpus for fine-grained opinion mining. *arXiv:1902.10102 [cs]*. ArXiv: 1902.10102.

Deepanway Ghosal, Md Shad Akhtar, Dushyant Chauhan, Soujanya Poria, Asif Ekbal, and Pushpak Bhattacharyya. 2018. Contextual Inter-modal Attention for Multi-modal Sentiment Analysis. In *Proceedings of the 2018 Conference on Empirical Methods in Natural Language Processing*, pages 3454–3466, Brussels, Belgium. Association for Computational Linguistics.

S. Gupta and R.J. Mooney. 2009. Using closed captions to train activity recognizers that improve video retrieval. In *Computer Vision and Pattern Recognition Workshops, 2009. CVPR Workshops 2009. IEEE Computer Society Conference on*, pages 30–37.

Sonal Gupta and Raymond J. Mooney. 2010. Using closed captions as supervision for video activity recognition. In *Proceedings of the Twenty-Fourth AAAI Conference on Artificial Intelligence (AAAI-2010)*, pages 1083–1088, Atlanta, GA.

Md Kamrul Hasan, Wasifur Rahman, AmirAli Bagher Zadeh, Jianyuan Zhong, Md Iftekhar Tanveer, Louis-Philippe Morency, and Mohammed (Ehsan) Hoque. 2019. UR-FUNNY: A multimodal language dataset for understanding humor. In *Proceedings of the 2019 Conference on Empirical Methods in Natural Language Processing and the 9th International Joint Conference on Natural Language Processing (EMNLP-IJCNLP)*, pages 2046–2056, Hong Kong, China. Association for Computational Linguistics.

Kaiming He, Xiangyu Zhang, Shaoqing Ren, and Jian Sun. 2016. Deep residual learning for image recognition. In *The IEEE Conference on Computer Vision and Pattern Recognition (CVPR)*.

Sergey Ioffe and Christian Szegedy. 2015. Batch normalization: Accelerating deep network training by reducing internal covariate shift. *arXiv preprint arXiv:1502.03167*.

Ozan Irsoy and Claire Cardie. 2014. Opinion Mining with Deep Recurrent Neural Networks. In *Proceedings of the 2014 Conference on Empirical Methods in Natural Language Processing (EMNLP)*, pages 720–728, Doha, Qatar. Association for Computational Linguistics.

Will Kay, João Carreira, Karen Simonyan, Brian Zhang, Chloe Hillier, Sudheendra Vijayanarasimhan, Fabio Viola, Tim Green, Trevor Back, Paul Natsev, Mustafa Suleyman, and Andrew Zisserman. 2017. The kinetics human action video dataset. *CoRR*.

Diederik P. Kingma and Jimmy Ba. 2014. Adam: A method for stochastic optimization. *CoRR*.

Amar Krishna, Joseph Zambreno, and Sandeep Krishnan. 2013. Polarity trend analysis of public sentiment on youtube. In *Proceedings of the 19th International Conference on Management of Data*, COMAD '13, pages 125–128, Mumbai, India, India. Computer Society of India.

Egor Lakomkin, Cornelius Weber, and Stefan Wermter. 2017. Automatically augmenting an emotion dataset improves classification using audio. In *Proceedings of the 15th Conference of the European Chapter of the Association for Computational Linguistics: Volume 2, Short Papers*, pages 194–197, Valencia, Spain. Association for Computational Linguistics.

Angeliki Lazaridou, Nghia The Pham, and Marco Baroni. 2015. Combining Language and Vision with a Multimodal Skip-gram Model. In *Proceedings of the 2015 Conference of the North American Chapter of the Association for Computational Linguistics: Human Language Technologies*, pages 153–163, Denver, Colorado. Association for Computational Linguistics.

Pengfei Liu, Shafiq Joty, and Helen Meng. 2015. Fine-grained Opinion Mining with Recurrent Neural Networks and Word Embeddings. In *Proceedings of the 2015 Conference on Empirical Methods in Natural Language Processing*, pages 1433–1443, Lisbon, Portugal. Association for Computational Linguistics.

Xuezhe Ma and Eduard Hovy. 2016. End-to-end Sequence Labeling via Bi-directional LSTM-CNNs-CRF. In *Proceedings of the 54th Annual Meeting of the Association for Computational Linguistics (Volume 1: Long Papers)*, pages 1064–1074, Berlin, Germany. Association for Computational Linguistics.

Edison Marrese-Taylor, Jorge Balazs, and Yutaka Matsuo. 2017. Mining fine-grained opinions on closed captions of YouTube videos with an attention-RNN. In *Proceedings of the 8th Workshop on Computational Approaches to Subjectivity, Sentiment and Social Media Analysis*, pages 102–111, Copenhagen, Denmark. Association for Computational Linguistics.

Grgoire Mesnil, Xiaodong He, Li Deng, and Yoshua Bengio. 2013. Investigation of recurrent-neural-network architectures and learning methods for spoken language understanding. In *INTERSPEECH*, pages 3771–3775.

Margaret Mitchell, Jacqui Aguilar, Theresa Wilson, and Benjamin Van Durme. 2013. Open Domain Targeted Sentiment. In *Proceedings of the 2013 Conference on Empirical Methods in Natural Language Processing*, pages 1643–1654, Seattle, Washington, USA. Association for Computational Linguistics.

Sunghyun Park, Han Suk Shim, Moitreya Chatterjee, Kenji Sagae, and Louis-Philippe Morency. 2014. Computational Analysis of Persuasiveness in Social Multimedia: A Novel Dataset and Multimodal Prediction Approach. In *Proceedings of the 16th International Conference on Multimodal Interaction*, ICMI '14, pages 50–57, New York, NY, USA. ACM.

Jeffrey Pennington, Richard Socher, and Christopher D. Manning. 2014. Glove: Global vectors for word representation. In *EMNLP*.

Hai Pham, Thomas Manzini, Paul Pu Liang, and Barnabs Poczs. 2018. Seq2seq2sentiment: Multimodal Sequence to Sequence Models for Sentiment Analysis. In *Proceedings of Grand Challenge and Workshop on Human Multimodal Language (Challenge-HML)*, pages 53–63, Melbourne, Australia. Association for Computational Linguistics.

Maria Pontiki, Dimitris Galanis, John Pavlopoulos, Harris Papageorgiou, Ion Androutsopoulos, and Suresh Manandhar. 2014. SemEval-2014 Task 4: Aspect Based Sentiment Analysis. In *Proceedings of the 8th International Workshop on Semantic Evaluation (SemEval 2014)*, pages 27–35, Dublin, Ireland. Association for Computational Linguistics and Dublin City University.

Soujanya Poria, Erik Cambria, and Alexander Gelbukh. 2015. Deep Convolutional Neural Network Textual Features and Multiple Kernel Learning for Utterance-level Multimodal Sentiment Analysis. In *Proceedings of the 2015 Conference on Empirical Methods in Natural Language Processing*, pages 2539–2544, Lisbon, Portugal. Association for Computational Linguistics.

Soujanya Poria, Erik Cambria, Devamanyu Hazarika, Navonil Majumder, Amir Zadeh, and Louis-Philippe Morency. 2017. Context-Dependent Sentiment Analysis in User-Generated Videos. In *Proceedings of the 55th Annual Meeting of the Association for Computational Linguistics (Volume 1: Long Papers)*, pages 873–883, Vancouver, Canada. Association for Computational Linguistics.

Aliaksei Severyn, Alessandro Moschitti, Olga Uryupina, Barbara Plank, and Katja Filippova. 2014. Opinion Mining on YouTube. In *Proceedings of the 52nd Annual Meeting of the Association for Computational Linguistics (Volume 1: Long Papers)*, pages 1252–1261, Baltimore, Maryland. Association for Computational Linguistics.

Stefan Siersdorfer, Sergiu Chelaru, Wolfgang Nejdl, and Jose San Pedro. 2010. How useful are your comments?: Analyzing and predicting youtube comments and comment ratings. In *Proceedings of the 19th International Conference on World Wide Web*, WWW '10, pages 891–900, New York, NY, USA. ACM.

Lucia Specia, Stella Frank, Khalil Sima'an, and Desmond Elliott. 2016. A Shared Task on Multimodal Machine Translation and Crosslingual Image Description. In *Proceedings of the First Conference on Machine Translation: Volume 2, Shared Task Papers*, pages 543–553, Berlin, Germany. Association for Computational Linguistics.

Christian Szegedy, Wei Liu, Yangqing Jia, Pierre Sermanet, Scott Reed, Dragomir Anguelov, Dumitru Erhan, Vincent Vanhoucke, and Andrew Rabinovich. 2015. Going deeper with convolutions. In *Proceedings of the IEEE conference on computer vision and pattern recognition*, pages 1–9.

Yasuyuki Tahara, Atsushi Tago, Hiroyuki Nakagawa, and Akihiko Ohsuga. 2010. Nicoscene: Video scene search by keywords based on social annotation. In Aijun An, Pawan Lingras, Sheila Petty, and Runhe Huang, editors, *Active Media Technology*, volume 6335 of *Lecture Notes in Computer Science*, pages 461–474. Springer Berlin Heidelberg.

Duyu Tang, Bing Qin, Xiaocheng Feng, and Ting Liu. 2016a. Effective LSTMs for Target-Dependent Sentiment Classification. In *Proceedings of COLING 2016, the 26th International Conference on Computational Linguistics: Technical Papers*, pages 3298–3307, Osaka, Japan. The COLING 2016 Organizing Committee.

Duyu Tang, Bing Qin, and Ting Liu. 2016b. Aspect Level Sentiment Classification with Deep Memory Network. In *Proceedings of the 2016 Conference on Empirical Methods in Natural Language Processing*, pages 214–224, Austin, Texas. Association for Computational Linguistics.

Du Tran, Lubomir Bourdev, Rob Fergus, Lorenzo Torresani, and Manohar Paluri. 2015. Learning spatiotemporal features with 3d convolutional networks. In *Proceedings of the IEEE international conference on computer vision*, pages 4489–4497.

Bin Wu, Erheng Zhong, Ben Tan, Andrew Horner, and Qiang Yang. 2014. Crowdsourced time-sync video tagging using temporal and personalized topic modeling. In *Proceedings of the 20th ACM SIGKDD International Conference on Knowledge Discovery and Data Mining*, KDD '14, pages 721–730, New York, NY, USA. ACM.

Huijuan Xu, Kun He, Bryan A. Plummer, Leonid Sigal, Stan Sclaroff, and Kate Saenko. 2018. Multilevel Language and Vision Integration for Text-to-Clip Retrieval. *arXiv:1804.05113 [cs]*. ArXiv: 1804.05113.

Liheng Xu, Kang Liu, and Jun Zhao. 2014. Joint Opinion Relation Detection Using One-Class Deep Neural Network. In *Proceedings of COLING 2014, the 25th International Conference on Computational Linguistics: Technical Papers*, pages 677–687, Dublin, Ireland. Dublin City University and Association for Computational Linguistics.

Jie Yang, Shuailong Liang, and Yue Zhang. 2018. Design Challenges and Misconceptions in Neural Sequence Labeling. In *Proceedings of the 27th International Conference on Computational Linguistics*, pages 3879–3889, Santa Fe, New Mexico, USA. Association for Computational Linguistics.

Jie Yang and Yue Zhang. 2018. NCRF++: An Open-source Neural Sequence Labeling Toolkit. In *Proceedings of ACL 2018, System Demonstrations*, pages 74–79, Melbourne, Australia. Association for Computational Linguistics.

Amir Zadeh, Minghai Chen, Soujanya Poria, Erik Cambria, and Louis-Philippe Morency. 2017. Tensor Fusion Network for Multimodal Sentiment Analysis. In *Proceedings of the 2017 Conference on Empirical Methods in Natural Language Processing*, pages 1103–1114, Copenhagen, Denmark. Association for Computational Linguistics.

Amir Zadeh, Rowan Zellers, Eli Pincus, and Louis-Philippe Morency. 2016. MOSI: Multimodal Corpus of Sentiment Intensity and Subjectivity Analysis in Online Opinion Videos. *arXiv:1606.06259 [cs]*. ArXiv: 1606.06259.

Meishan Zhang, Yue Zhang, and Duy Tin Vo. 2015. Neural Networks for Open Domain Targeted Sentiment. In *Proceedings of the 2015 Conference on Empirical Methods in Natural Language Processing*, pages 612–621, Lisbon, Portugal. Association for Computational Linguistics.

Xin Zhao, Jing Jiang, Hongfei Yan, and Xiaoming Li. 2010. Jointly modeling aspects and opinions with a MaxEnt-LDA hybrid. In *Proceedings of the 2010 Conference on Empirical Methods in Natural Language Processing*, pages 56–65, Cambridge, MA. Association for Computational Linguistics.

Y. Zuo, J. Wu, H. Zhang, D. Wang, and K. Xu. 2018. Complementary aspect-based opinion mining. *IEEE Transactions on Knowledge and Data Engineering*, 30(2):249–262.

Multilogue-Net: A Context Aware RNN for Multi-modal Emotion Detection and Sentiment Analysis in Conversation

Aman Shenoy[*]
Birla Inst. of Technology and Science, Pilani
Pilani, RA, India
f2016393@pilani.bits-pilani.ac.in

Ashish Sardana
NVIDIA Graphics
Bengaluru, KA, India
asardana@nvidia.com

Abstract

Sentiment Analysis and Emotion Detection in conversation is key in several real-world applications, with an increase in modalities available aiding a better understanding of the underlying emotions. Multi-modal Emotion Detection and Sentiment Analysis can be particularly useful, as applications will be able to use specific subsets of available modalities, as per the available data. Current systems dealing with Multi-modal functionality fail to leverage and capture - the context of the conversation through all modalities, the dependency between the listener(s) and speaker emotional states, and the relevance and relationship between the available modalities. In this paper, we propose an end to end RNN architecture that attempts to take into account all the mentioned drawbacks. Our proposed model, at the time of writing, out-performs the state of the art on a benchmark dataset on a variety of accuracy and regression metrics.

1 Introduction

Multi-modal Emotion Detection and Sentiment Analysis in conversation is gathering a lot of attention recently considering its potential use cases owing to the rapid growth of online social media platforms such as YouTube, Facebook, Instagram, Twitter etc. (Chen et al., 2017, Poria et al., 2016, Poria et al., 2017, Zadeh et al., 2016b, Zadeh et al., 2017), especially knowing that information obtained from any combination of more than one of the available modalities (e.g. text, audio, video) can be used to produce meaningful results.

The current state of the art systems on multi-modal emotion detection and sentiment analysis do not treat the modalities in accordance to the information they are capable of holding (e.g. textual information is significantly more likely to hold

contextual information then audio or video features are), lack an adequate fusion mechanism, and fail to effectively capture the context of a conversation in a multi-modal setting. In addition to the lack of proper usage of the available modalities, models also fail to effectively capture the flow of a conversation, the separation between speaker and listener states, and the emotional effect a speaker's utterance has on the listener (s) in dyadic conversations.

Our proposed model Multilogue-Net, attempts to embed basic domain knowledge and takes insight from Poria et al. (2019), assuming that the sentiment or emotion governing a particular utterance predominantly depends on 4 factors – interlocutor state, interlocutor intent, the preceding and future emotions, and the context of the conversation. Interlocutor intent amongst the mentioned is particularly difficult to model due to its dependency of prior knowledge about the speaker, but modelling the other 3 separately, yet in an interrelated manner was theorized to produce meaningful results if managed to be captured effectively. The key intention was to attempt to simulate the setting in which an utterance is said, and use the actual utterance at that point to be able to gain better insights regarding emotion and sentiment of that utterance. The model uses information from all modalities learning multiple state vectors (representing interlocutor state) for a given utterance, followed by a pairwise attention mechanism inspired by Ghosal et al. (2018), attempting to better capture the relationship between all pairs of the available modalities.

The model uses two gated recurrent units (GRU) (Chung et al., 2014) for each modality for modelling interlocutor state and emotion. Along with these GRU's, the model also uses an interconnected context network, consisting of the same number of GRU's as the number of available modalities, to model a different learned context representation for each modality. The incoming utterance

---

[*] The following work was pursued when author was an intern at NVIDIA Graphics, Bengaluru

19

Proceedings of the 58th Annual Meeting of the Association for Computational Linguistics, pages 19–28
Seattle, USA, July5 - 10, 2020. ©2017 Association for Computational Linguistics
https://doi.org/10.18653/v1/P17

representations and the historical GRU outputs are used at every timestamp to be able to arrive at a prediction for that timestamp.

The model produces m different representations at every timestamp (Where m is the number of modalities), where each representation is the emotional state at that timestamp as conveyed by each of the modalities. These m representations are used by the fusion mechanism to incorporate information from each of the m representations to be able to arrive at the final prediction for that timestamp. We understand that the usage of the pairwise attention mechanism, along with the Emotion GRU are what make the model flexible across tasks.

The usage of only the text representation as input to the context GRU's has been observed to be key to the results, as the context of the conversation would be better captured by textual information then it would have with audio or video information. We believe that Multilogue-net performs better than the current state of the art (Ghosal et al., 2018) on multi-modal datasets because of better context representation leveraging all available modalities.[1]

The remaining sections of the paper are arranged as follows: Section 2 – discusses related work; Section 3 – discusses the model in detail; Section 4 – provides experimental results, dataset details, and analysis; Section 5 contains our ablation studies and its implications; and finally Section 6 – speaks on potential future work, and concludes our paper.

2　Related Work

Multi-modal Emotion recognition and Sentiment Analysis has always attracted attention in multiple fields such as natural language processing, psychology, cognitive science, and so on (Picard, 2010). Previous works have been done studying factors of variation that have a more direct correlation with emotion, such as Ekman et al. (1992), who found correlation between emotion and facial cues, and a lot of studies extensively focus on emotions and their relationship with one another such as Plutchik's wheel of emotions, which defines eight primary emotion types, each of which has a multitude of emotions as sub-types.

Early work done to leverage multi-modal information for emotion recognition includes works such as Datcu and Rothkrantz (2012), who fused acoustic information with visual cues for emotion recognition and Eyben et al. (2010), who used contextual information for emotion recognition in multi-modal settings. More recently, deep recurrent neural networks have been used to be able make the best of the learned representations of the modalities available to be able to give very effective and accurate emotion and sentiment predictions. Poria et al. (2017) successfully used RNN-based deep networks for multi-modal emotion recognition, which was followed by multiple other works (Chen et al., 2017; Zadeh et al., 2018a; Zadeh et al., 2018c) giving results far better than what was seen before. Recent works also include works such as Hazarika et al. (2018), who used memory networks for emotion recognition in dyadic conversations, where two distinct memory networks enabled inter-speaker interaction.

Some works such as DialogueRNN (Majumder et al., 2018), though focused on emotion recognition and sentiment analysis using a single modality (text), works very well in a multi-modal setting by just replacing the text representation with a concatenated vector of all the modality representations. DialogueRNN effectively leveraged the separation between the speakers by maintaining two independent gated recurrent units to keep track of the interlocutor states, also effectively capturing context in the conversation, yielding state-of-the-art performance on uni-modal data. Even though DialogueRNN was able to give reasonably good results on multi-modal data, the lack of an adequate fusion mechanism and the lack of focus on a multi-modal representation held its multi-modal performance back.

Apart from the kind of works shown before, where a methodology or a model was proposed, works such as Poria et al. (2019) spoke extensively about the research challenges and advancements in emotion detection in conversation and gave a comprehensive overview of the problem. Most recently Ghosal et al. (2018) introduced the idea of learning the relationship between pairs of all available modalities using pairwise attention, in a multi-modal setting, where similar attributes learned by multiple modalities are emphasized and differences between the modality representations are diminished. Pairwise attention proved to be incredibly effective yielding state-of-the-art performance on multi-modal data with just simple representations for each modality.

---

[1] A basic model and training implementation of Multilogue-Net can be found at `https://github.com/amanshenoy/multilogue-net`.

3 Proposed Methodology

3.1 Problem Formulation

Let there be a P number of participants $p_1, p_2, ..., p_P$ in the conversation. The problem is defined such that for every utterance $u_1, u_2, ..., u_N$ uttered by any participant(s), a sentiment score is allotted along with a predicted emotion label (one of happy, sad, angry, surprise, disgust, and fear). Each utterance corresponds to a particular participant of the conversation, allowing this formulation of the problem to also capture the average sentiment of a participant in the conversation. Predictions over utterances also avoid problems such as classification during long moments of silence when predictions are made for a fixed time interval, and is also mostly common practice.

For every utterance $u_t(p)$, where p is the party who uttered the utterance, there exist three independent representations , $t_t \in \mathbb{R}^{D_t}$, $a_t \in \mathbb{R}^{D_a}$, and $v_t \in \mathbb{R}^{D_v}$, and are obtained using the feature extractors further explained in section 4.2.

This gives us our overall formulation of the problem, which is to be able to learn a function which would take as input three independent representations of a particular utterance, information regarding the previous emotional state of the participant, and a representation of the current context of the conversation - to be able to map to an output prediction of a sentiment score and emotion label.

Details regarding how these representations are updated and how the output is generated using these inputs are described in detail below.

3.2 Model Details

Modelling was done under the underlying assumption that the sentiment or emotion of an utterance predominantly depends on four factors as mentioned before:

- Interlocutor State

- Interlocutor Intent

- Context of the conversation until that point

- Previous interlocutor states and emotions of a particular participant in the conversation

The proposed model attempts to model three out of the mentioned four explicitly, and assume that interlocutor intent will be modelled implicitly during model training. Interlocutor state is modelled using a state GRU (will be referred to as $sGRU$),

A context GRU is used to keep track of the context of the conversation ($cGRU$), and an emotion GRU ($eGRU$) is used to keep track of the emotional state of that particular participant. Finally, a pairwise attention mechanism, which uses the emotion representation of all modalities at a particular timestamp is used to leverage the important modalities and relevant combination of the modalities for emotion or sentiment prediction at that timestamp.

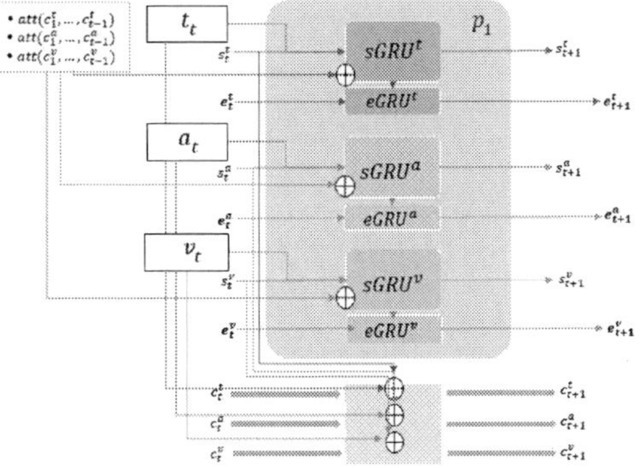

Figure 1: Description of all the state updates at timestamp t for a single participant p_1

Every utterance has three independent feature representations (text, audio, and video features), $t_t \in \mathbb{R}^{D_t}$, $a_t \in \mathbb{R}^{D_a}$, and $v_t \in \mathbb{R}^{D_v}$. Each of these feature representations are treated and operated on independently until the pairwise attention mechanism. The model consists of two GRU's (state GRU, and emotion GRU) for every modality and participant, and a context GRU for each modality common to all participants in the conversation (If p is the number of participants and m is the number of modalities, the model would have a total of $2mp + m$ GRU's). The inputs at the current timestamp and the previous state, context, and emotion representations are operated on to be able to arrive at the prediction at that timestamp. Figure 1 describes the updates at a particular timestamp and the role of each GRU is further explained below.

3.2.1 Context GRU ($cGRU$)

The Context GRU ($cGRU$) for each modality aims to capture the context of the conversation by jointly encoding the utterance representation of that modality (at timestamp t in the given diagram) ($t_t \in \mathbb{R}^{D_t}$, $a_t \in \mathbb{R}^{D_a}$, or $v_t \in \mathbb{R}^{D_v}$) and the previous timestamp speaker state GRU output of that modality. This accounts for inter-speaker and inter-utterance dependencies to produce an effective context rep-

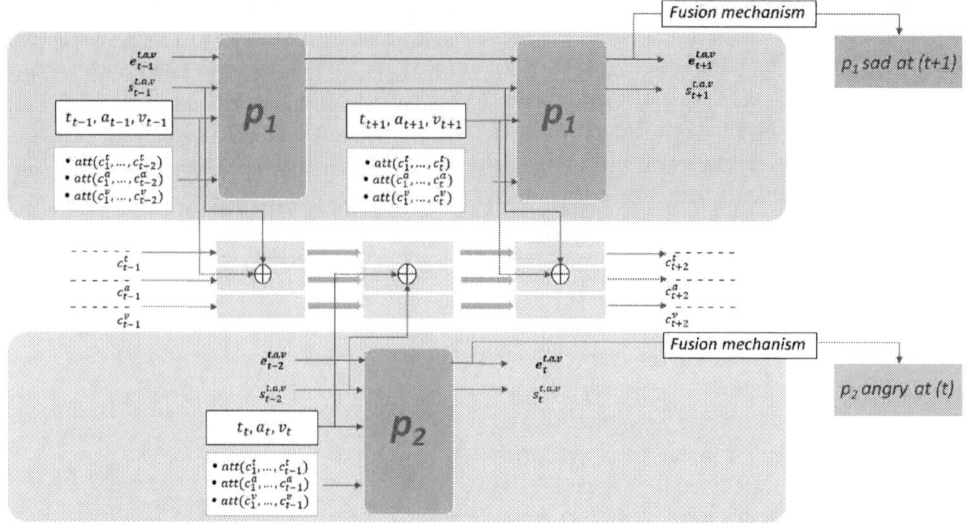

Figure 2: State updates and final prediction output in a conversation between two participants p_1 and p_2, where the updates of each participant at a timestamp is as given in figure 1

resentation. The current utterance t_t, a_t, or v_t, changes the state of that speaker from (s_t^t, s_t^a, s_t^v) to $(s_{t+1}^t, s_{t+1}^a, s_{t+1}^v)$. To capture this change in context we use GRU cell $cGRU$ having output size D_c, using t_t, a_t, or v_t and (s_t^t, s_t^a, s_t^v) as:

$$c_{t+1}^t = cGRU(c_t^t, (t_t \oplus s_t^t)) \tag{1}$$

$$c_{t+1}^a = cGRU(c_t^a, (a_t \oplus s_t^a)) \tag{2}$$

$$c_{t+1}^v = cGRU(c_t^v, (v_t \oplus s_t^v)) \tag{3}$$

Where D_c is the size of the context vectors c_{t+1}^t, c_{t+1}^a, and c_{t+1}^v. D_t, D_a, and D_v are the sizes of utterance representations of text, audio, and video respectively. $\oplus$ represents the concatenation operation, D_s is the size of all the state vectors s_{t+1}^t, s_{t+1}^a, and s_{t+1}^v; and all GRU weight and biases shapes are such that they produce the expected shape of outputs taking the given shape of inputs.

3.2.2 State GRU ($sGRU$)

The network keeps track of the participants involved in a conversation by employing a $p * m$ number of ($sGRU$)'s, where p is the number participants in the conversation and m is the number of available modalities. The $sGRU$ associated with a participant outputs fixed size vectors which serve as an encoding to represent the interlocutor state,

and are directly used for both emotion and sentiment prediction, and updating the context vectors.

All the state vectors are initialized to null at the first timestamp. For a timestamp t, the state vector of participant p and modality $m \in \{t, a, v\}$ is updated using the input feature representation of that modality and simple attention over all the context vectors until that timestamp. The simple attention mechanism over all the context vectors is described by the following equations:

$$\alpha = softmax(m_t^T W_\alpha [c_1^m, c_2^m, ..., c_t^m]) \tag{4}$$

$$att_t = \alpha [c_1^m, c_2^m, ..., c_t^m]^T \tag{5}$$

Where $m_t^T \in \{t_t^T, a_t^T, v_t^T\}$, $W_\alpha \in \mathbb{R}^{D_{t,a,v} \times D_c}$, $\alpha^T \in \mathbb{R}^{(t-1)}$, and $att_t \in \mathbb{R}^{D_c}$. In equation 4, we calculate attention scores over all previous context representations of all previous utterances, highlighting the relative importance of all the previous context vectors to m_t. A softmax layer is applied to amplify this relative importance, and finally equation 5 the final output of attention over context att_t is calculated by pooling the previous context vectors with α.

We then employ $sGRU^{t,a,v}$ to update $s_t^{t,a,v}$ to $s_{t+1}^{t,a,v}$ on the basis of incoming utterance representations for each modality $m_t^T \in \{t_t^T, a_t^T, v_t^T\}$ and the context representations att_t^t, att_t^a, and att_t^v using

GRU cells $sGRU_t^t$, $sGRU_t^a$, and $sGRU_t^v$, each of output size D_s.

$$s_{t+1}^t = sGRU(s_t^t, (t_t \oplus att_{t+1}^t)) \tag{6}$$

$$s_{t+1}^a = sGRU(s_t^a, (a_t \oplus att_{t+1}^a)) \tag{7}$$

$$s_{t+1}^v = sGRU(s_t^v, (v_t \oplus att_{t+1}^v)) \tag{8}$$

Where D_s is the size of all the state vectors s_{t+1}^t, s_{t+1}^a, and s_{t+1}^v. D_t, D_a, D_v are the sizes of utterance representations of text, audio, and video respectively. $\oplus$ represents concatenation operation, and all GRU weights shapes are such that they produce the expected shape of outputs taking the given shape of inputs.

The intended purpose of using this as the input to $sGRU^{t,a,v}$ is to model the dependency of the speaker state on the context of the conversation as understood by the utterances until that point, along with the utterance representation at that point. The output of the $sGRU$ for modality m and timestamp t serves as an encoding of the speaker state as conveyed by modality m, at time t.

3.2.3 Emotion GRU ($eGRU$)

The emotion GRU serves as the decoder for the encoding produced by the state GRU. The emotion GRU uses the previous timestamp $eGRU$ output, and the encoding provided by $sGRU$ to produce an emotion or sentiment representation which is further used by the pairwise attention mechanism to be able to produce the relevant output for prediction. At timestamp $(t+1)$ the emotion vectors are updated as:

$$e_{t+1}^t = eGRU(e_t^t, s_{t+1}^t) \tag{9}$$

$$e_{t+1}^a = eGRU(e_t^a, s_{t+1}^a) \tag{10}$$

$$e_{t+1}^v = eGRU(e_t^v, s_{t+1}^v) \tag{11}$$

Where D_e is the size of all the emotion vectors e_{t+1}^t, e_{t+1}^a, and e_{t+1}^v. $D_t, D_a, and D_v$ are the sizes of utterance representations of text, audio, and video respectively. D_e is the size of the state vectors s_{t+1}^t, s_{t+1}^a, and s_{t+1}^v; and all GRU weights shapes are such that they produce the expected shape of outputs taking the given shape of inputs.

The emotion GRU acts as a decoder to the encoding produced by the associated state GRU, producing a vector which can be used for both sentiment and emotion prediction.

3.2.4 Pairwise Attention Mechanism

The emotion GRU for each timestamp will produce an m number of vectors (where m is the number of modalities available). Pairwise attention is then used over these m vectors to produce the final prediction output. In particular pairwise attention is calculated over the following pairs in our case – $(e^v, e^t), (e^t, e^a)$, and (e^a, e^v). Pairwise attention for pair (e^v, e^t) would be calculated as follows:

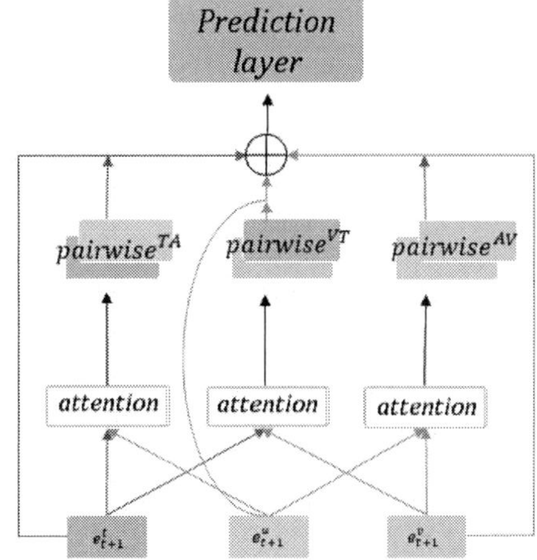

Figure 3: Pairwise attention mechanism used as the fusion mechanism followed by the final prediction layer

$$B_1 = e^v.(e^t)^T, B_2 = e^t.(e^v)^T \tag{12}$$

$$N_1 = softmax(B_1), N_2 = softmax(B_2) \tag{13}$$

$$O_1 = N_1.e^t, O_2 = N_2.e^v \tag{14}$$

$$A_1 = O_1 \odot e^v, A_2 = O_2 \odot e^t \tag{15}$$

$$pairwise(e^v, e^t) = A_1 \oplus A_2 \tag{16}$$

Where $B_1, B_2 \in \mathbb{R}^{D_e \times D_e}$; $N_1, N_2 \in \mathbb{R}^{D_e \times D_e}$; $A_1, A_2 \in \mathbb{R}^{D_e \times D_e}$; and $pairwise(e^v, e^t) \in \mathbb{R}^{D_e \times 2D_e}$; $\odot$ represents element-wise product; and $\oplus$ represents concatenation.

A complete analysis on the pairwise attention mechanism has been done by Ghosal et al. (2018), where the role of each one of the intermediate variables has been described. These equations (12, 13, 14, 15, 16) calculate $^mC_2$ pairwise fusion representations, which are further concatenated to make the final prediction as described below.

3.2.5 Final Predictions

The prediction layer varies based on whether a sentiment or emotion prediction is expected. For sentiment prediction first all three pairs of pairwise attention i.e. $pairwise(e^v, e^t)$, $pairwise(e^a, e^t)$, and $pairwise(e^v, e^a)$ at that timestamp are concatenated along with the emotion GRU outputs at that timestamp (e_t^t, e_t^a, and e_t^v) and the concatenated layer is passed through a fully connected layer followed by a $softmax$ or $tanh$ layer based on the nature of the expected prediction. For sentiment prediction between -1 and +1 at timestamp t the output layer would equate as follows:

$$pw = pw(e^v, e^t) \oplus pw(e^a, e^t) \oplus pw(e^v, e^a) \quad (17)$$

$$L_t = pw \oplus e_t^t \oplus e_t^a \oplus e_t^v \quad (18)$$

$$pred_{sentiment(t)} = tanh(W_L L_t) \quad (19)$$

Where $pairwise(e^v, e^t)$ has been represented as $pw(e^v, e^t)$; and $W_L \in \mathbb{R}^{9D_e \times 1}$.

For emotion prediction we use a fully connected layer along with a final $softmax$ layer to calculate 6 emotion class probabilities from L_t.

$$l_t = ReLU(W_l L_t + b_l) \quad (20)$$

$$P_t = softmax(W_{smax} l_t + b_{smax}) \quad (21)$$

$$pred_{emotion(t)} = argmax(P_t) \quad (22)$$

Where $W_l \in \mathbb{R}^{D_l \times 9D_e}$; $b_l = \in \mathbb{R}^{D_l}$; $W_{smax} \in \mathbb{R}^{c \times D_l}$; $b_{smax} \in \mathbb{R}^c$ and $P_t \in \mathbb{R}^c$

3.2.6 Training

Fairly standard practices have been employed for the training of the model. Categorical cross-entropy has been used along with L2-regularization as the loss function during training for emotion prediction, to maximize likelihood over each of the classes.

Mean Square Error (MSE) along with L2 regularization has been employed as loss function during training for sentiment regression. The usage of a

Metric	A2	F1
Text + Audio		
BC-LSTM	79.30	-
MMMU-BA	**80.58**	-
DialogueRNN	78.81	**79.12**
Multilogue-net	80.12	78.84
Video + Audio		
BC-LSTM	62.10	-
MMMU-BA	65.16	-
DialogueRNN	63.22	60.14
Multilogue-net	**69.55**	**63.40**
Text + Video		
BC-LSTM	80.20	-
MMMU-BA	**81.51**	-
DialogueRNN	79.88	79.10
Multilogue-net	80.66	**79.62**
Text + Audio + Video		
BC-LSTM	80.30	-
MMMU-BA	**82.31**	-
DialogueRNN	79.80	79.48
Multilogue-net	81.19	**80.10**

Table 1: Multilogue-Net performance on CMU-MOSI in comparison with the current and previous state-of-the-art on the dataset. A2 indicating accuracy with 2 classes, and F1 indicating F1 score .

saturating output layer and a loss function that does not undo the saturation, leads to the model to stop training when it makes extreme predictions (close to -1 or +1) due to very small gradients. Using initialization strategies that start at smaller model weights, mini-batch gradient descent-based Adam (Kingma and Ba, 2014) optimizer, and using L2 regularization is used to avoid this failure mode.

4 Experiments, Datasets, and Results

4.1 Datasets

We evaluate our model using two benchmark datasets - CMU Multi-modal Opinion-level Sentiment Intensity (CMU-MOSI) (Zadeh et al., 2016a) and the recently published CMU Multi-modal Opinion Sentiment and Emotion Intensity (CMU-MOSEI) dataset (Zadeh et al., 2018b).

4.1.1 CMU-MOSI

CMU-MOSI dataset consists of 93 videos spanning over 2199 utterances. Each utterance has a sentiment label associated with it. It has 52, 10 & 31 videos in training, validation & test set accounting for 1151, 296 & 752 utterances. CMU-MOSEI has 3229 videos with 22676 utterances from more than 1000 online YouTube speakers. The training, validation & test set consist of 16216, 1835 & 4625 utterances, respectively. Each utterance in CMU-MOSI dataset has been annotated as either positive or negative.

4.1.2 CMU-MOSEI

In CMU-MOSEI dataset labels are in a continuous range of -3 to +3 and are accompanied by an emotion label being one of six emotions. However, in this work we also project the instances of CMU-MOSEI in a two-class classification setup with values ≥ 0 signifies positive sentiments and values < 0 signify negative sentiments. We have called this A2 accuracy (accuracy with 2 classes). Along with this we have also shown results for continuous range prediction between -3 and +3, and emotion prediction with the 6 emotion labels for each utterance in CMU- MOSEI. We have used A2 as a metric to be consistent with the previous published works on CMU-MOSEI dataset (Ghosal et al., 2018; Zadeh et al., 2018b). CMU-MOSEI has further been used for other comprehensive experiments due to its large sizer and easier feature extraction

4.2 Uni-modal Feature Extraction

4.2.1 CMU-MOSEI

We use the CMU-Multi-modal Data SDK (Zadeh et al., 2018b) for feature extraction. For MOSEI dataset, sentiment label-level features were provided where text features used were GloVe embeddings (Pennington et al., 2014), visual features extracted by Facet (Stöckli et al., 2017) & acoustic features by OpenSMILE (Eyben et al., 2010). Thereafter, we compute the average of sentiment label-level features in an utterance to obtain the utterance-level features. For each sentiment label-level feature, the dimension of the feature vector is set to 300 (text), 35 (visual) & 384 (acoustic).

4.2.2 CMU-MOSI

In contrast, for MOSI dataset we use utterance level features provided in Poria et al. (2017). These utterance-level features represent the outputs of a convolutional neural network (Karpathy et al., 2014), 3D convolutional neural network (Ji et al., 2010) & openSMILE (Eyben et al., 2010) for text, visual & acoustic modalities, respectively. Dimensions of utterance-level features are 100, 100 & 73 for text, visual & acoustic, respectively.

Metric	A2	F1	MAE	r
T + A				
MMMU-BA	79.74	-	-	-
DialogueRNN	79.80	78.32	-	-
Multilogue-net	**80.18**	**79.88**	-	-
V + A				
MMMU-BA	**76.66**	-	-	-
DialogueRNN	73.90	73.92	-	-
Multilogue-net	75.16	**74.04**	-	-
V + T				
MMMU-BA	79.40	-	-	-
DialogueRNN	78.90	78.12	-	-
Multilogue-net	**80.06**	**79.84**	-	-
T + A + V				
Graph-MFN	76.90	77.00	0.71	**0.54**
MMMU-BA	79.80	-	-	-
DialogueRNN	79.98	79.82	0.69	0.42
Multilogue-net	**82.10**	**80.01**	**0.59**	0.50

Table 2: Multilogue-Net performance on CMU-MOSEI Sentiment Labels compared to previous state-of-the-art models on regression and accuracy Metrics. All metrics apart from MAE represents higher values for better results, MAE represents lower values for better results.

4.3 Experiments

We evaluate our proposed approach on CMU-MOSI (test-set) on accuracy and F1 score, and CMU-MOSEI (dev-set) on accuracy, F1 score, mean absolute error (MAE), pearson score (r), and accuracy's on the emotion labels. Due to the lack of speaker information in CMU-MOSI we were not able to use the CMU-Multi-modal Data SDK for sentiment label extraction, to be able to evaluate our approach on CMU-MOSI on mean absolute error and Pearson score.

Results have also been reported for usage of two of the three available modalities. Uni-modal performance has not been reported as the focus of the paper is the effective usage of multi-modal data. In a uni-modal setting the model would not be using the fusion mechanism and the output would be equivalent to having a few dense layers after the emotion GRU to directly output the final prediction. F1 scores have not been mentioned by most previous models being used for comparison, but have been reported for Multilogue-Net for additional comparison to any future models using CMU-MOSI dataset.

Table 1 shows the performance of Multilogue-

MOSEI Emotions (Text + Video + Audio)												
Emotion	Anger		Disgust		Fear		Happy		Sad		Surprise	
Metric	WA	F1	WA	F1	WA	F1	WA	F1	WA	F1	WA	F1
Graph-MFN	62.6	72.8	69.1	76.6	62.0	**89.9**	66.3	66.3	60.4	66.9	53.7	**85.5**
Multilogue-Net	**83.1**	**80.9**	**90.3**	**87.3**	**89.7**	87.0	**70.0**	**68.4**	**76.1**	**74.5**	**87.4**	84.0

Table 3: Multilogue-Net performance on MOSEI Emotion Labels compared with that of Graph-MFN on weighted accuracy and F1 score. MOSEI Emotion label results were presented by only one model, and comprehensive results have not been published for the same.

Net on CMU-MOSI dataset, comparing to the current state of the art (Ghosal et al., 2018), previous state-of-the-art (Poria et al., 2017), and DialogueRNN (Majumder et al., 2018) (Multi-modal performance of DialogueRNN has not been reported by Majumder et al. (2018), and we have run these experiments additionally for a better comparative study, where concatenating the input representations has been used as a fusion mechanism). Our model consistently outperforms the previous state-of-the-art but performs better only on one of the subsets of the modalities when compared to the current state-of-the-art.

In comparison to MMMU-BA our model also lacks in Multi-modal performance. We theorize that the model performance is lacking because of the low number of training examples (CMU-MOSI consists only of 93 conversations out of which 62 were used for training), in contrast to our model which has a high capacity (Relative to models being compared with). Since Multilogue-Net learns a lot of intermediate representations in order to make a prediction, it would need a larger dataset with more variability to be able to learn meaningful representations. The proposition that performance lacks due to a lack of training examples is backed by the results on CMU-MOSEI (demonstrated in a comparative setting in Table 2 and 3) where the model consistently outperforms the current state-of-the-art on most metrics.

On CMU-MOSEI, our model seems to perform very consistently on both sentiment and emotion labels. The model outperforms the current state of the art on all but one metric (both classification and accuracy) on sentiment labels in the tri-modal setting. Multilogue-Net also outperforms the current state of the art on the emotion labels by a considerable margin (This is also attributed to the fact that not a lot of models have presented results on these labels).

Similar observations are made in both datasets,

where the tri-modal metrics show the best performance, and audio + video show the worst relative performance (suggesting the importance of text in a multi-modal setting). Textual information seems to be the guiding factor for multi-modal performance, with video and audio features simply acting as a push to the uni-modal performance on text.

We theorize that the performance of Multilogue-Net is majorly attributed to its increased capacity as compared to previous models. Effective usage of this increased capacity, using representations inspired from a basic understanding of conversation, along with a larger dataset for training have been key in achieving the improved results.

5   Ablation Studies and Analysis

Until now, some architectural considerations, such as the use of $eGRU$ and the fusion mechanism, have been briefly explained but not empirically justified. This section aims to get empirical evidence regarding the effectiveness of these modules. Since our model completely hinges around the usage of the context and state GRU's, our ablation studies and analysis have focused on the fusion mechanism and emotion GRU ($eGRU$) only.

5.1   Fusion Mechanism

The effectiveness of the fusion mechanism can be very easily examined by observing the results of the model on both tasks — Sentiment Regression and Emotion Recognition, with and without the fusion mechanism. Table 4 shows these results on CMU-MOSEI modality subsets.

The bi-modal results in table 4 involve evaluating the pairwise attention module only once (Since there is only one pair available), directly followed by the prediction layer. The tri-modal case on the other hand involves evaluating the pairwise attention module thrice (Once for each pair). In general, the number of times this module will have to be evaluated for m modalities is $^{m}C_2$, which raises

Fusion Mechanism	A2	MAE
Text + Audio		
without	75.78	-
with	**80.18**	-
Video + Audio		
without	**75.66**	-
with	75.16	-
Text + Video		
without	76.80	-
with	**80.06**	-
Text + Audio + Video		
without	79.80	0.66
with	**82.10**	**0.59**

Table 4: Multilogue-Net performance on CMU-MOSEI with and without the fusion mechanism - for 'without' fusion we have concatenated all the representations and directly passed them to the prediction layer.

Representation	Euclidean Distance
Sample 6 with $t = 4$	
s_4^t	4.6 units
c_4^t	6.1 units
e_4^t	26.4 units

Table 5: Euclidean Distance between the same representations for Sentiment Regression as compared to Emotion Detection. (Distances have been converted to units for convenience and easier comparison)

a fair concern regarding the trade-off between the additional computational cost and performance.

We empirically observe that the additional computational cost can be considered negligible in context of the increased performance, largely attributing to the non-parametric nature of the fusion mechanism and the relatively small number of additional parameters in the prediction layer ($6D_e$ for the sentiment regression; $36D_e$ for emotion recognition).

The fusion mechanism seems to clearly be beneficial in all of the reported cases apart from video + audio, implying that the fusion mechanism is useful only in the cases the text representation is used. This further strengthens our claim that the text representation guides tri-modal performance.

5.2 Emotion GRU ($eGRU$)

Unlike as done with the fusion mechanism, the effectiveness of the $eGRU$ cannot be examined by evaluating metrics with and without it. Removing the Emotion GRU would clearly be detrimental to the results, and would not convey the intention of having it.

The primary intention of having the $eGRU$ can be considered to be maintaining consistency between tasks. To better understand what this means table 5 quantitatively demonstrates this effect. The model was trained separately for Emotion Detection and Sentiment Regression tasks. After both the models were trained satisfactorily, a particular sample from the test set (test sample 6) was inferred on. We then retrieved the intermediate text representations (e_4^t, c_4^t, and s_4^t; superscript t indicating text modality) at a particular timestamp ($t = 4$) for both models on that sample. The Euclidean Distance between these two sets of representations (one for each task) was evaluated and have been shown in table 5, where we can clearly observe that the euclidean distance between the emotion representations is much larger as compared to the state and context representations.

This shows that for both tasks, interlocutor state and context representations are relatively similar to each other, whereas the emotion state representation is more varied and task dependant. This not only allows us to use the same $cGRU$ and $sGRU$ weights across tasks, but would also allow us to train for multiple tasks in parallel using a different $eGRU$ for each task - giving us consistent and accurate predictions across multiple tasks. Analysis of such a network, and whether training for multiple tasks in parallel aids one another, has not been covered in this paper and is left to our future work.

6 Conclusion

In this paper, we have presented an RNN architecture for multi-modal sentiment analysis and emotion detection in conversation. In contrast to the current state-of-the-art models, our model focuses on effectively capturing the context of a conversation and treats each modality independently, taking into account the information a particular modality is capable of holding. Our model consistently performs well on benchmark datasets such as CMU-MOSI and CMU-MOSEI in any multi-modal setting.

The model can be further extended to have better feature extractors, and increase both the number of modalities and the number of participants in the conversation. Due to the lack of availability of datasets consisting of these extensions with emotion or sentiment labels, we have left this to our future work.

References

Minghai Chen, Sen Wang, Paul Pu Liang, Tadas Baltrušaitis, Amir Zadeh, and Louis-Philippe Morency. 2017. Multimodal sentiment analysis with word-level fusion and reinforcement learning. In *Proceedings of the 19th ACM International Conference on Multimodal Interaction*, pages 163–171.

Junyoung Chung, Caglar Gulcehre, KyungHyun Cho, and Y. Bengio. 2014. Empirical evaluation of gated recurrent neural networks on sequence modeling.

Dragos Datcu and Léon Rothkrantz. 2012. Semantic audiovisual data fusion for automatic emotion recognition.

P. Ekman, Edmund Rolls, David Perrett, and H. Ellis. 1992. Facial expressions of emotion: An old controversy and new findings: Discussion. *Royal Society of London Philosophical Transactions Series B*, 335:69–.

Florian Eyben, Martin Wöllmer, and Björn Schuller. 2010. opensmile – the munich versatile and fast open-source audio feature extractor. pages 1459–1462.

Deepanway Ghosal, Md Shad Akhtar, Dushyant Chauhan, Soujanya Poria, and Pushpak Bhattacharyya Asif Ekbal. 2018. Contextual inter-modal attention for multi-modal sentiment analysis. In *Proceedings of the 2018 Conference on Empirical Methods in Natural Language Processing*, pages 3454–3466.

Devamanyu Hazarika, Soujanya Poria, Amir Zadeh, Erik Cambria, Louis-Philippe Morency, and Roger Zimmermann. 2018. Conversational memory network for emotion recognition in dyadic dialogue videos. volume 2018, pages 2122–2132.

Shuiwang Ji, Wei Xu, Ming Yang, and Kai Yu. 2010. 3d convolutional neural networks for human action recognition. volume 35, pages 495–502.

Andrej Karpathy, George Toderici, Sanketh Shetty, Thomas Leung, Rahul Sukthankar, and Li Fei-Fei. 2014. Large-scale video classification with convolutional neural networks. pages 1725–1732.

Diederik Kingma and Jimmy Ba. 2014. Adam: A method for stochastic optimization. *International Conference on Learning Representations*.

Navonil Majumder, Soujanya Poria, Devamanyu Hazarika, Rada Mihalcea, Alexander Gelbukh, and Erik Cambria. 2018. Dialoguernn: An attentive rnn for emotion detection in conversations.

Jeffrey Pennington, Richard Socher, and Christoper Manning. 2014. Glove: Global vectors for word representation. volume 14, pages 1532–1543.

Rosalind Picard. 2010. Affective computing: From laughter to ieee. *IEEE Transactions on Affective Computing*, 1:11–17.

Soujanya Poria, Erik Cambria, Devamanyu Hazarika, Navonil Majumder, Amir Zadeh, and Louis-Philippe Morency. 2017. Context-dependent sentiment analysis in user-generated videos. In *Proceedings of the 55th Annual Meeting of the Association for Computational Linguistics*, pages 873–883.

Soujanya Poria, Iti Chaturvedi, Erik Cambria, and Amir Hussain. 2016. Convolutional mkl based multimodal emotion recognition and sentiment analysis. In *IEEE 16th International Conference on Data Mining (ICDM)*, pages 439–448.

Soujanya Poria, Navonil Majumder, Rada Mihalcea, and Eduard Hovy. 2019. Emotion recognition in conversation: Research challenges, datasets, and recent advances. *arXiv:1905.02947*.

Sabrina Stöckli, Michael Schulte-Mecklenbeck, Stefan Borer, and Andrea Samson. 2017. Facial expression analysis with affdex and facet: A validation study. *Behavior Research Methods*, 50.

Amir Zadeh, Minghai Chen, Soujanya Poria, Erik Cambria, and Louis-Philippe Morency. 2017. Tensor fusion network for multimodal sentiment analysis. In *Proceedings of the 2017 Conference on Empirical Methods in Natural Language Processing*, pages 1103–1114.

Amir Zadeh, Paul Liang, Navonil Mazumder, Soujanya Poria, Erik Cambria, and Louis-Philippe Morency. 2018a. Memory fusion network for multi-view sequential learning.

Amir Zadeh, Paul Liang, Soujanya Poria, Erik Cambria, and Louis-Philippe Morency. 2018b. Multimodal language analysis in the wild: Cmu-mosei dataset and interpretable dynamic fusion graph. pages 2236–2246.

Amir Zadeh, Paul Liang, Soujanya Poria, Prateek Vij, Erik Cambria, and Louis-Philippe Morency. 2018c. Multi-attention recurrent network for human communication comprehension. *Proceedings of the 2018 AAAI Conference on Artificial Intelligence*, 2018.

Amir Zadeh, Rowan Zellers, Eli Pincus, and Louis-Philippe Morency. 2016a. Mosi: Multimodal corpus of sentiment intensity and subjectivity analysis in online opinion videos.

Amir Zadeh, Rowan Zellers, Eli Pincus, and Louis-Philippe Morency. 2016b. Multimodal sentiment intensity analysis in videos: Facial gestures and verbal messages. *Intelligent Systems, IEEE*, pages 82–88.

Low Rank Fusion based Transformers for Multimodal Sequences

Saurav Sahay   Eda Okur   Shachi H Kumar   Lama Nachman
Intel Labs, Anticipatory Computing Lab, USA
{saurav.sahay, eda.okur, shachi.h.kumar, lama.nachman}
@intel.com

Abstract

Our senses individually work in a coordinated fashion to express our emotional intentions. In this work, we experiment with modeling modality-specific sensory signals to attend to our latent multimodal emotional intentions and vice versa expressed via low-rank multimodal fusion and multimodal transformers. The low-rank factorization of multimodal fusion amongst the modalities helps represent approximate multiplicative latent signal interactions. Motivated by the work of (Tsai et al., 2019) and (Liu et al., 2018), we present our transformer-based cross-fusion architecture without any over-parameterization of the model. The low-rank fusion helps represent the latent signal interactions while the modality-specific attention helps focus on relevant parts of the signal. We present two methods for the Multimodal Sentiment and Emotion Recognition results on CMU-MOSEI, CMU-MOSI, and IEMOCAP datasets and show that our models have lesser parameters, train faster and perform comparably to many larger fusion-based architectures.

1   Introduction

The field of Emotion Understanding involves computational study of subjective elements such as sentiments, opinions, attitudes, and emotions towards other objects or persons. Subjectivity is an inherent part of emotion understanding that comes from the contextual nature of the natural phenomenon. Defining the metrics and disentangling the objective assessment of the metrics from the subjective signal makes the field quite challenging and exciting. Sentiments and Emotions are attached to the language, audio and visual modalities at different rates of expression and granularity and are useful in deriving social, psychological and behavioral insights about various entities such as movies, products, people or organizations. Emotions are defined as brief organically synchronized evaluations of major events whereas sentiments are considered as more enduring beliefs and dispositions towards objects or persons (Scherer, 1984). The field of Emotion Understanding has rich literature with many interesting models of understanding (Plutchik, 2001; Ekman, 2009; Posner et al., 2005). Recent studies on tensor-based multimodal fusion explore regularizing tensor representations (Liang et al., 2019) and polynomial tensor pooling (Hou et al., 2019).

In this work, we combine ideas from (Tsai et al., 2019) and (Liu et al., 2018) and explore the use of Transformer (Vaswani et al., 2017) based models for both aligned and unaligned signals without extensive over-parameterization of the models by using multiple modality-specific transformers. We utilize Low Rank Matrix Factorization (LMF) based fusion method for representing multimodal fusion of the modality-specific information. Our main contributions can be summarized as follows:

- Recently proposed Multimodal Transformer (MulT) architecture (Tsai et al., 2019) uses at least 9 Transformer based models for cross-modal representation of language, audio and visual modalities (3 parallel modality-specific standard Transformers with self-attention and 6 parallel bimodal Transformers with cross-modal attention). These models utilize several parallel unimodal and bimodal transformers and do not capture the full trimodal signal interplay in any single transformer model in the architecture. In contrast, our method uses fewer Transformer based models and fewer parallel models for the same multimodal representation.

- We look at two methods for leveraging the multimodal fusion into the transformer architecture. In one method (LMF-MulT), the fused multimodal signal is reinforced using

29

Proceedings of the 58th Annual Meeting of the Association for Computational Linguistics, pages 29–34
Seattle, USA, July5 - 10, 2020. ©2017 Association for Computational Linguistics
https://doi.org/10.18653/v1/P17

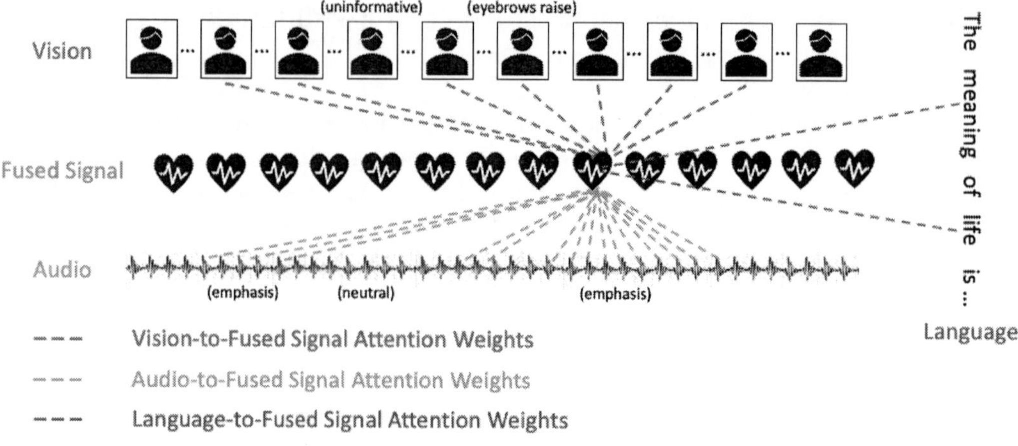

Figure 1: Modality-specific Fused Attention

attention from the 3 modalities. In the other method (Fusion-Based-CM-Attn), the individual modalities are reinforced in parallel via the fused signal.

The ability to use unaligned sequences for modeling is advantageous since we rely on learning based methods instead of using methods that force the signal synchronization (requiring extra timing information) to mimic the coordinated nature of human multimodal language expression. The LMF method aims to capture all unimodal, bimodal and trimodal interactions amongst the modalities via approximate Tensor Fusion method.

We develop and test our approaches on the CMU-MOSI, CMU-MOSEI, and IEMOCAP datasets as reported in (Tsai et al., 2019). CMU Multimodal Opinion Sentiment and Emotion Intensity (CMU-MOSEI) (Zadeh et al., 2018) is a large dataset of multimodal sentiment analysis and emotion recognition on YouTube video segments. The dataset contains more than 23,500 sentence utterance videos from more than 1000 online YouTube speakers. The dataset has several interesting properties such as being gender balanced, containing various topics and monologue videos from people with different personality traits. The videos are manually transcribed and properly punctuated. Since the dataset comprises of natural audio-visual opinionated expressions of the speakers, it provides an excellent test-bed for research in emotion and sentiment understanding. The videos are cut into continuous segments and the segments are annotated with 7 point scale sentiment labels and 4 point scale emotion categories corresponding to the Ekman's 6 basic emotion classes (Ekman, 2002). The opinionated expressions in the segments contain visual cues, audio variations in signal as well as textual expressions showing various subtle and non-obvious interactions across the modalities for both sentiment and emotion classification. CMU-MOSI (Zadeh et al., 2016) is a smaller dataset (2199 clips) of YouTube videos with sentiment annotations. IEMOCAP (Busso et al., 2008) dataset consists of 10K videos with sentiment and emotion labels. We use the same setup as (Tsai et al., 2019) with 4 emotions (happy, sad, angry, neutral).

In Fig 1, we illustrate our ideas by showing the fused signal representation attending to different parts of the unimodal sequences. There's no need to align the signals since the attention computation to different parts of the modalities acts as proxy to the multimodal sequence alignment. The fused signal is computed via Low Rank Matrix Factorization (LMF). The other model we propose uses a swapped configuration where the individual modalities attend to the fused signal in parallel.

2 Model Description

In this section, we describe our models and methods for Low Rank Fusion of the modalities for use with Multimodal Transformers with cross-modal attention.

2.1 Low Rank Fusion

LMF is a Tensor Fusion method that models the unimodal, bimodal and trimodal interactions without using an expensive 3-fold Cartesian product (Zadeh et al., 2017) from modality-specific embeddings.

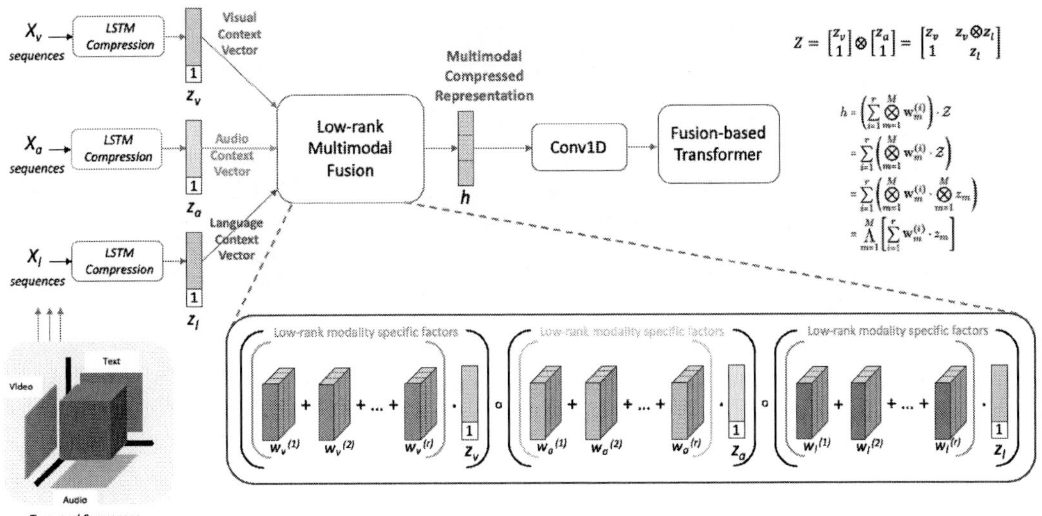

Figure 2: Low Rank Matrix Factorization

Instead, the method leverages unimodal features and weights directly to approximate the full multitensor outer product operation. This low-rank matrix factorization operation easily extends to problems where the interaction space (feature space or number of modalities) is very large. We utilize the method as described in (Liu et al., 2018). Similar to the prior work, we compress the time-series information of the individual modalities using an LSTM (Hochreiter and Schmidhuber, 1997) and extract the hidden state context vector for modality-specific fusion. We depict the LMF method in Fig 2 similar to the illustration in (Liu et al., 2018). This shows how the unimodal tensor sequences are appended with 1s before taking the outer product to

be equivalent to the tensor representation that captures the unimodal and multimodal interaction information explicitly (top right of Fig 2). As shown, the compressed representation (h) is computed using batch matrix multiplications of the low-rank modality-specific factors and the appended modality representations. All the low-rank products are further multiplied together to get the fused vector.

2.2 Multimodal Transformer

We build up on the Transformers (Vaswani et al., 2017) based sequence encoding and utilize the ideas from (Tsai et al., 2019) for multiple cross-modal attention blocks followed by self-attention for encoding multimodal sequences for classifi-

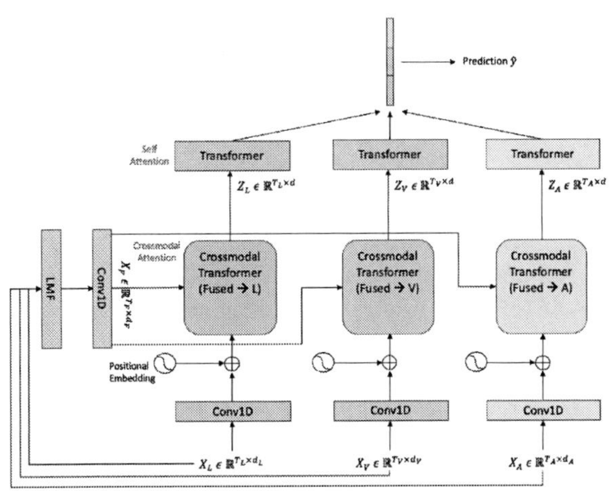

Figure 3: Fused Cross-modal Transformer

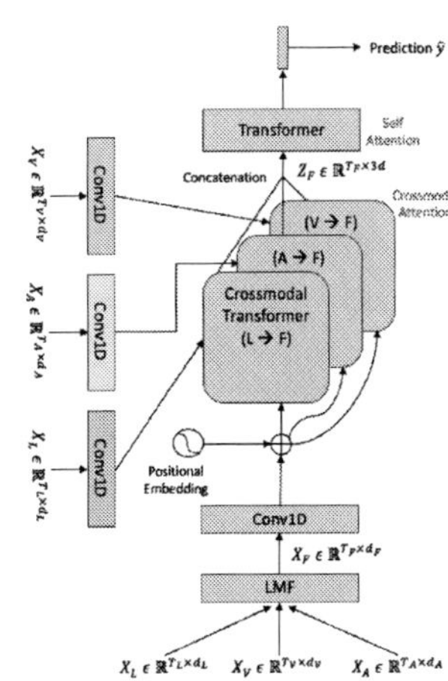

Figure 4: Low Rank Fusion Transformer

Metric	Acc_7^h	Acc_2^h	F1^h	MAE^l	Corr^h
(Aligned) CMU-MOSI Sentiment					
LF-LSTM (pub)	35.3	76.8	76.7	1.015	0.625
MulT (Tsai et al., 2019) (pub)	40.0	83.0	82.8	0.871	0.698
MulT (Tsai et al., 2019) (our run)	**33.1**	**78.5**	**78.4**	**0.991**	**0.676**
Fusion-Based-CM-Attn-MulT (ours)	32.9	77.0	76.9	1.017	0.636
LMF-MulT (ours)	32.4	77.9	77.9	1.016	0.647
(Unaligned) CMU-MOSI Sentiment					
LF-LSTM (pub)	33.7	77.6	77.8	0.988	0.624
MulT (Tsai et al., 2019) (pub)	39.1	81.1	81.0	0.889	0.686
MulT (Tsai et al., 2019) (our run)	34.3	**80.3**	**80.4**	1.008	0.645
Fusion-Based-CM-Attn-MulT (ours)	**34.4**	76.8	76.8	1.003	0.640
LMF-MulT (ours)	34.0	78.5	78.5	**0.957**	**0.681**

Table 1: Performance Results for Multimodal Sentiment Analysis on CMU-MOSI dataset with aligned and unaligned multimodal sequences.

Metric	Acc_7^h	Acc_2^h	F1^h	MAE^l	Corr^h
(Aligned) CMU-MOSEI Sentiment					
LF-LSTM (pub)	48.8	80.6	80.6	0.619	0.659
MulT (Tsai et al., 2019) (pub)	51.8	82.5	82.3	0.580	0.703
MulT (Tsai et al., 2019) (our run)	49.3	**80.5**	**81.1**	0.625	0.663
Fusion-Based-CM-Attn-MulT (ours)	49.6	79.9	80.7	**0.616**	**0.673**
LMF-MulT (ours)	**50.2**	80.3	80.3	**0.616**	0.662
(Unaligned) CMU-MOSEI Sentiment					
LF-LSTM (pub)	48.8	77.5	78.2	0.624	0.656
MulT (Tsai et al., 2019) (pub)	50.7	81.6	81.6	0.591	0.694
MulT (Tsai et al., 2019) (our run)	**50.4**	80.7	80.6	0.617	**0.677**
Fusion-Based-CM-Attn-MulT (ours)	49.3	79.4	79.2	**0.613**	0.674
LMF-MulT (ours)	49.3	**80.8**	**81.3**	0.620	0.668

Table 2: Performance Results for Multimodal Sentiment Analysis on larger-scale CMU-MOSEI dataset with aligned and unaligned multimodal sequences.

cation. While the earlier work focuses on latent adaptation of one modality to another, we focus on adaptation of the latent multimodal signal itself using single-head cross-modal attention to individual modalities. This helps us reduce the excessive parameterization of the models by using all combinations of modality to modality cross-modal attention for each modality. Instead, we only utilize a linear number of cross-modal attention for each modality and the fused signal representation. We add Temporal Convolutions after the LMF operation to ensure that the input sequences have a sufficient awareness of the neighboring elements. We show the overall architecture of our two proposed models in Fig 3 and Fig 4. In Fig 3, we show the fused multimodal signal representation after a temporal convolution to enrich the individual modalities via cross-modal transformer attention. In Fig 4, we show the architecture with the least number of Transformer layers where the individual modalities attend to the fused convoluted multimodal signal.

3 Experiments

We present our early experiments to evaluate the performance of proposed models on the standard multimodal datasets used by (Tsai et al., 2019)[1]. We run our models on CMU-MOSI, CMU-MOSEI, and IEMOCAP datasets and present the results for the proposed LMF-MulT and Fusion-Based-CM-Attn-MulT models. Late Fusion (LF) LSTM is a common baseline for all datasets with reported results (pub) together with MulT in (Tsai et al., 2019). We include the results we obtain (our run) for the MulT model for a direct comparison[2]. Table 1, Table 2, and Table 3 show the performance of various models on the sentiment analysis and emotion classification datasets. We do not observe any trend suggesting that our methods can achieve better accuracies or F1-scores than the original MulT method (Tsai et al., 2019). However, we do note

---

[1] We have built this work up on the code-base released for MulT (Tsai et al., 2019) at `https://github.com/yaohungt/Multimodal-Transformer`

[2] In this work, we have not focused on the further hyperparameter tuning of our models.

Emotion	Happy		Sad		Angry		Neutral	
Metric	Acc^h	$F1^h$	Acc^h	$F1^h$	Acc^h	$F1^h$	Acc^h	$F1^h$
(Aligned) IEMOCAP Emotions								
LF-LSTM (pub)	85.1	86.3	78.9	81.7	84.7	83.0	67.1	67.6
MulT (Tsai et al., 2019) (pub)	90.7	88.6	86.7	86.0	87.4	87.0	72.4	70.7
MulT (Tsai et al., 2019) (our run)	**86.4**	82.9	82.3	82.4	85.3	85.8	**71.2**	70.0
Fusion-Based-CM-Attn-MulT (ours)	85.6	83.7	83.6	**83.7**	84.6	85.0	70.4	69.9
LMF-MulT (ours)	85.3	**84.1**	**84.1**	83.4	**85.7**	**86.2**	71.2	**70.8**
(Unaligned) IEMOCAP Emotions								
LF-LSTM (pub)	72.5	71.8	72.9	70.4	68.6	67.9	59.6	56.2
MulT (Tsai et al., 2019) (pub)	84.8	81.9	77.7	74.1	73.9	70.2	62.5	59.7
MulT (Tsai et al., 2019) (our run)	**85.6**	**79.0**	**79.4**	**70.3**	**75.8**	**65.4**	59.2	44.0
Fusion-Based-CM-Attn-MulT (ours)	**85.6**	**79.0**	**79.4**	**70.3**	**75.8**	**65.4**	**59.3**	**44.2**
LMF-MulT (ours)	**85.6**	**79.0**	**79.4**	**70.3**	**75.8**	**65.4**	59.2	44.0

Table 3: Performance Results for Multimodal Emotion Recognition on IEMOCAP dataset with aligned and unaligned multimodal sequences.

Dataset	CMU-MOSI		CMU-MOSEI		IEMOCAP	
Model	Aligned	Unaligned	Aligned	Unaligned	Aligned	Unaligned
MulT (Tsai et al., 2019)	18.87	19.25	191.40	216.32	36.20	37.93
Fusion-Based-CM-Attn (ours)	14.53	15.80	140.95	175.68	26.10	29.16
LMF-MulT (ours)	**11.01**	**12.03**	**106.15**	**137.35**	**20.57**	**23.53**

Table 4: Average Time/Epoch (sec)

Dataset	CMU-MOSI	CMU-MOSEI	IEMOCAP
MulT (Tsai et al., 2019)	1071211	1073731	1074998
Fusion-Based-CM-Attn (ours)	**512121**	**531441**	**532078**
LMF-MulT (ours)	836121	855441	856078

Table 5: Number of Model Parameters

that on some occasions, our methods can achieve higher results than the MulT model, in both aligned (see LMF-MulT results for IEMOCAP in Table 3) and unaligned (see LMF-MulT results for CMU-MOSEI in Table 2) case. We plan to do an exhaustive grid search over the hyper-parameters to understand if our methods can learn to classify the multimodal signal better than the original competitive method. Although the results are comparable, below are the advantages of using our methods:

- Our LMF-MulT model does not use multiple parallel self-attention transformers for the different modalities and it uses least number of transformers compared to the other two models. Given the same training infrastructure and resources, we observe a consistent speedup in training with this method. See Table 4 for average time per epoch in seconds measured with fixed batch sizes for all three models.

- As summarized in Table 5, we observe that our models use lesser number of trainable parameters compared to the MulT model, and yet achieve similar performance.

4 Conclusion

In this paper, we present our early investigations towards utilizing Low Rank representations of the multimodal sequences for usage in multimodal transformers with cross-modal attention to the fused signal or the modalities. Our methods build up on the (Tsai et al., 2019) work and apply transformers to fused multimodal signal that aim to capture all inter-modal signals via the Low Rank Matrix Factorization (Liu et al., 2018). This method is applicable to both aligned and unaligned sequences. Our methods train faster and use fewer parameters to learn classifiers with similar SOTA performance. We are exploring methods to compress the temporal sequences without using the hidden state context vectors from LSTMs that lose the temporal information. We recover the temporal information with a Convolution layer. We believe these models can be deployed in low resource settings with further optimizations. We are also interested in using richer features for the audio, text, and the vision pipeline for other use-cases where we can utilize more resources.

References

Carlos Busso, Murtaza Bulut, Chi-Chun Lee, Abe Kazemzadeh, Emily Mower, Samuel Kim, Jeannette N. Chang, Sungbok Lee, and Shrikanth S. Narayanan. 2008. Iemocap: interactive emotional dyadic motion capture database. *Language Resources and Evaluation*, 42(4):335.

Paul Ekman. 2002. Facial action coding system (facs). *A Human Face*.

Paul Ekman. 2009. *Telling Lies: Clues to Deceit in the Marketplace, Politics, and Marriage (Revised Edition)*. WW Norton & Company.

Sepp Hochreiter and Jürgen Schmidhuber. 1997. Long short-term memory. *Neural Computation*, 9(8):1735–1780.

Ming Hou, Jiajia Tang, Jianhai Zhang, Wanzeng Kong, and Qibin Zhao. 2019. Deep multimodal multilinear fusion with high-order polynomial pooling. In H. Wallach, H. Larochelle, A. Beygelzimer, F. dAlché-Buc, E. Fox, and R. Garnett, editors, *Advances in Neural Information Processing Systems 32*, pages 12136–12145. Curran Associates, Inc.

Paul Pu Liang, Zhun Liu, Yao-Hung Hubert Tsai, Qibin Zhao, Ruslan Salakhutdinov, and Louis-Philippe Morency. 2019. Learning representations from imperfect time series data via tensor rank regularization. In *Proceedings of the 57th Annual Meeting of the Association for Computational Linguistics*, pages 1569–1576, Florence, Italy. Association for Computational Linguistics.

Zhun Liu, Ying Shen, Varun Bharadhwaj Lakshminarasimhan, Paul Pu Liang, AmirAli Bagher Zadeh, and Louis-Philippe Morency. 2018. Efficient low-rank multimodal fusion with modality-specific factors. *Proceedings of the 56th Annual Meeting of the Association for Computational Linguistics (Volume 1: Long Papers)*.

Robert Plutchik. 2001. The nature of emotions human emotions have deep evolutionary roots, a fact that may explain their complexity and provide tools for clinical practice. *American Scientist*.

Jonathan Posner, James A Russell, and Bradley S Peterson. 2005. The circumplex model of affect: An integrative approach to affective neuroscience, cognitive development, and psychopathology. *Development and psychopathology*, 17(03):715–734.

Klaus R Scherer. 1984. Emotion as a multicomponent process: A model and some cross-cultural data. *Review of Personality & Social Psychology*.

Yao-Hung Hubert Tsai, Shaojie Bai, Paul Pu Liang, J. Zico Kolter, Louis-Philippe Morency, and Ruslan Salakhutdinov. 2019. Multimodal transformer for unaligned multimodal language sequences. In *Proceedings of the 57th Annual Meeting of the Association for Computational Linguistics (Volume 1: Long Papers)*, Florence, Italy. Association for Computational Linguistics.

Ashish Vaswani, Noam Shazeer, Niki Parmar, Jakob Uszkoreit, Llion Jones, Aidan N Gomez, Ł ukasz Kaiser, and Illia Polosukhin. 2017. Attention is all you need. In I. Guyon, U. V. Luxburg, S. Bengio, H. Wallach, R. Fergus, S. Vishwanathan, and R. Garnett, editors, *Advances in Neural Information Processing Systems 30*, pages 5998–6008. Curran Associates, Inc.

Amir Zadeh, Minghai Chen, Soujanya Poria, Erik Cambria, and Louis-Philippe Morency. 2017. Tensor fusion network for multimodal sentiment analysis. *CoRR*, abs/1707.07250.

Amir Zadeh, Paul Pu Liang, Jon Vanbriesen, Soujanya Poria, Erik Cambria, Minghai Chen, and Louis-Philippe Morency. 2018. Multimodal language analysis in the wild: Cmu-mosei dataset and interpretable dynamic fusion graph. In *Association for Computational Linguistics (ACL)*.

Amir Zadeh, Rowan Zellers, Eli Pincus, and Louis-Philippe Morency. 2016. Multimodal sentiment intensity analysis in videos: Facial gestures and verbal messages. *IEEE Intelligent Systems*, 31(6):82–88.

Unsupervised Online Grounding of Natural Language during Human-Robot Interactions

Oliver Roesler
Artificial Intelligence Lab
Vrije Universiteit Brussel
Brussels, Belgium
`oliver@roesler.co.uk`

Abstract

Allowing humans to communicate through natural language with robots requires connections between words and percepts. The process of creating these connections is called symbol grounding and has been studied for nearly three decades. Although many studies have been conducted, not many considered grounding of synonyms and the employed algorithms either work only offline or in a supervised manner. In this paper, a cross-situational learning based grounding framework is proposed that allows grounding of words and phrases through corresponding percepts without human supervision and online, i.e. it does not require any explicit training phase, but instead updates the obtained mappings for every new encountered situation. The proposed framework is evaluated through an interaction experiment between a human tutor and a robot, and compared to an existing unsupervised grounding framework. The results show that the proposed framework is able to ground words through their corresponding percepts online and in an unsupervised manner, while outperforming the baseline framework.

1 Introduction

An increasing number of service robots is employed in human-centered complex environments and interacts with humans on a regular basis. This creates a need for robots that are able to understand instructions provided in natural language, such as *bring a glas of water* or *pick up a box*, to execute them appropriately and thereby enable efficient collaboration with humans. To this end, connections between words, i.e. abstract symbols, and their corresponding percepts, i.e. meanings, need to be created because according to the "Symbol Grounding Problem", which was proposed in 1990 by Harnad (1990), abstract knowledge and language only has meaning, if it is linked to the physical world through mappings from words to corresponding percepts.

Grounding approaches can in general be separated into supervised and unsupervised approaches. The former utilize the guidance of a human tutor, while the latter do not require any supervision and try to use co-occurrence information to identify through which percepts a word is grounded. Previous studies, such as (Kollar et al., 2010; Tellex et al., 2011; Aly and Taniguchi, 2018), that investigated unsupervised grounding employed algorithms that only work offline, i.e. these algorithms need to be trained before deployment with in advance collected perceptual data and words, which prevents these algorithms from being used in real-time human-robot interactions. Additionally, most previous studies did not consider ambiguous words, although the sentences humans produce are often ambiguous due to homonymy, i.e. one word refers to several percepts, and synonymy, i.e. one percept can be referred to by several different words. The latter do not need to be true synonyms, i.e. words that refer to the exact same meaning, instead, words only need to be synonyms as references to a percept in a particular set of situations, e.g. *coca cola* or *lemonade* instead of *bottle*.

In this paper, a recently proposed unsupervised online grounding framework (Roesler and Nowé, 2019) is extended to handle real percepts obtained during human-robot interactions. More specifically, the learning framework is extended to first convert obtained percepts through clustering to an abstract representation, which is then used to ground all non-auxiliary words[1] of the encountered natural language instructions through cross-situational learning. Each shape, color, and action is referred to by at least two synonymous words, which need to

---

[1] Auxiliary words are words that do not have corresponding percepts and only exist for grammatical reasons.

Proceedings of the 58th Annual Meeting of the Association for Computational Linguistics, pages 35–45
Seattle, USA, July5 - 10, 2020. ©2017 Association for Computational Linguistics
https://doi.org/10.18653/v1/P17

be mapped to their corresponding geometric characteristics, color histograms, or kinematic features of the robot joints during action execution, to investigate the ability of the used frameworks to handle synonymous words. The grounding performance of the proposed framework is evaluated by comparing it to the grounding performance of a Bayesian grounding framework that has been used in several previous studies, e.g. (Aly and Taniguchi, 2018; Roesler et al., 2018, 2019)

The rest of this paper is structured as follows: Sections (2 and 3) provide a brief overview of cross-situational learning and related work. Afterwards, an overview of the proposed unsupervised online grounding framework as well as the unsupervised Bayesian baseline framework is given in Sections (4 and 5). The experimental design and obtained results are described in Sections (6 and 7). Finally, Section (8) concludes the paper.

2 Background

Cross-situational learning (CSL) refers to the process of learning the meaning of words across multiple exposures to handle referential uncertainty. The basic idea is that a set of candidate meanings, i.e. mappings from words to percepts, can be created for every situation or context a word is used in and that the correct meaning can be obtained by determining the intersection of the sets of candidate meanings (Pinker, 1989; Fisher et al., 1994). Thus, the correct mapping between a word and its corresponding percepts, i.e. its meaning, will reliably reoccur across situations (Blythe et al., 2010; Smith and Smith, 2012). A number of experimental studies have confirmed that humans use CSL for word learning, when no prior knowledge of language is available (Akhtar and Montague, 1999; Gillette et al., 1999; Smith and Yu., 2008). Since CSL requires more than one exposure to learn a word, it belongs to the group of slow-mapping mechanisms through which most words are acquired (Carey, 1978). In contrast, *fast-mapping* allows words to be acquired through a single exposure, but it is only used for a limited number of words and can neither be explained nor achieved through CSL (Carey and Bartlett, 1978; Vogt, 2012). Many different algorithms have been proposed to simulate CSL in humans and enable artificial agents, such as robots, to learn the meaning of words by grounding them through percepts (Section 3).

3 Related Work

Grounding is used to obtain the meaning of an abstract symbol, e.g. a word, by linking it to perceptual information, i.e. the "real" world (Harnad, 1990). There exist many different approaches for grounding. She et al. (2014) grounded higher level symbols through already grounded lower level symbols with the help of a dialog system. Since the system requires a sufficiently large set of grounded lower level symbols as well as a professional tutor to answer its questions, its usefulness is limited. The need for a human tutor that knows the correct mappings also limits the applicability of the *Naming Game*, which allows an agent to quickly learn word-percept mappings (Steels and Loetzsch, 2012). In contrast to the previous approaches, cross-situational learning (Section 2), which assumes that one word appears several times together with the same perceptual feature vector so that a corresponding mapping can be created, does not require a human tutor for grounding (Siskind, 1996; Smith et al., 2011). Previous studies investigated the use of cross-situational learning for grounding of objects, actions, and spatial concepts (Roesler et al., 2019; Dawson et al., 2013). In most studies, grounding was conducted offline, i.e. perceptual data and words were collected in advance, which prevents these approaches from being used in real-time human-robot interactions. In contrast to these approaches, the framework used in this study learns the correct mappings from words to percepts online while interacting with humans and does not require separate training and test phases. Additionally, the majority of employed models were not able to handle ambiguous words, although, the sentences humans produce are often ambiguous due to homonymy and synonymy. One recent study showed that grounding of known synonyms does not require semantic or syntactic information and that such information can even have a negative effect, depending on the characteristics of the used information and how it is applied (Roesler et al., 2018). Therefore, the online grounding mechanism employed in this study uses no additional semantic or syntactic information to ground synonyms.

4 Grounding Framework

The employed grounding framework consists of four parts: (1) 3D object segmentation component, which segments objects into point clouds to determine their geometric characteristics and colors, (2)

Action recording component, which creates action feature vectors by recording the states of several joints while the robot is executing actions, (3) Percept clustering component, which obtains an abstract representation of percepts through clustering, and (4) Cross-situational learning based grounding component, which identifies auxiliary words and maps percepts to non-auxiliary words and phrases. The inputs and outputs of the individual parts are highlighted below, and described in detail in the following subsections.

1. **3D object segmentation**:

   - **Input**: Point cloud data.
   - **Output**: Geometric characteristics and colors of objects.

2. **Action recording**:

   - **Input**: Changes of the robot's joint states during action execution.
   - **Output**: Action feature vectors representing the executed actions.

3. **Clustering of percepts**:

   - **Input**: Geometric object characteristics, object colors, and action feature vectors.
   - **Output**: Cluster numbers of percepts.

4. **Cross-situational learning**:

   - **Input**: Natural language instructions and cluster numbers of percepts.
   - **Output**: Word to percept mappings.

4.1 3D Object Features

In this study, an unsupervised model based 3D point cloud segmentation approach is used to segment objects lying in a plane into separate point clouds because it is fast, reliable and does not need much prior knowledge, such as object models or the number of regions to process (Craye et al., 2016). The applied model uses the RANSAC algorithm (Fischler and Bolles, 1981) to detect the major plane in the environment, which is a tabletop in the conducted experiment, and keeps track of it in consecutive frames. If a plane is orthogonal to the major plane and touches at least one border of the image, it is defined as a wall plane. After filtering out points that belong to the main plane or wall planes, the remaining points are voxelized and clustered into blobs representing object candidates. Blobs that are neither extremely small nor large are

Figure 1: Illustration of the used objects and the corresponding 3D point cloud information: (A) car, (B) bottle, and (C) cup.

treated as objects[2]. Point clouds of segmented objects are characterized through Viewpoint Feature Histogram (VFH) descriptors (Rusu et al., 2010), which represent the object geometries taking into consideration the viewpoints while ignoring scale variances, and color histograms, which represent the colors of the objects. Figure (1) provides an illustrative example of the obtained 3D point cloud information.

4.2 Action Features

Action feature vectors are used to represent the dynamic characteristics of actions during execution through teleoperation. Overall, five different characteristics, which represent possible subactions, are recorded through the sensors of the robot (Toyota Motor Corporation, 2017). The used characteristics are:

1. The distance from the actual to the lowest torso position in meters.

2. The angle of the arm flex joint in radians.

3. The angle of the wrist roll joint in radians.

4. Velocity of the base.

5. Binary state of the gripper (1: closing, 0: opening or no change).

They are then combined into the following vector:

$$\begin{pmatrix} a_1^1 & a_1^2 & a_1^3 & a_1^4 & a_1^5 \\ \vdots & \vdots & \vdots & \vdots & \vdots \\ a_6^1 & a_6^2 & a_6^3 & a_6^4 & a_6^5 \end{pmatrix},$$

where a^1 represents the difference of the distances from the lowest torso position in meters, while a^2 and a^3 represent the differences in the angles of the arm flex and wrist roll joints in radians, respectively. The differences are calculated by subtracting the

---

[2]The threshold for the blob size was manually set based on the objects used in the experiment and should be suitable for all objects of similar size.

values at the beginning of the subaction from the values at the end of the subaction. a^4 represents the mean velocity of the base (forward/backward), and a^5 represents the binary gripper state. Each action is characterized through six manually defined subactions. Therefore, if an action consists of less than six subactions, rows with zeros are added at the end, while the duration of a subaction is not fixed because it depends on the teleoperator.

4.3 Clustering of percepts

The CSL algorithm (Section 4.4) requires percepts to be converted to an abstract representation that can then be used to ground natural language. The abstract representation is obtained through clustering as proposed in (Roesler, 2019). Since it cannot be assumed that the number of clusters, i.e. the number of different percepts, is known in advance, DBSCAN, which is a density-based clustering algorithm proposed by Ester et al. (1996), is used[3] because it determines the number of clusters automatically, while only requiring two parameters, i.e. the radius ϵ and threshold *minSamples*. Each iteration DBSCAN determines a number of core points, which are points that have more than *minSamples* points within radius ϵ around them (Schubert et al., 2017). All the points within radius ϵ of a core point are assigned to the same cluster as the core point. Cluster numbers are calculated every situation prior to grounding so that they can be provided to the CSL algorithm. Recalculating them every situation is necessary to take into account the new percepts of that situation.

4.4 Cross-Situational Learning

A variety of algorithms have been developed that realize CSL in different ways, e.g. through the use of probabilistic models (Aly and Taniguchi, 2018; Roesler et al., 2019), to ground words through percepts in artificial agents. This section describes an online CSL algorithm for grounding of words, which has first been proposed by Roesler and Nowé (2018) and recently been extended with auxiliary word and phrase detection (Roesler and Nowé, 2019). Since the sentences in this study are shorter, have a much simpler structure, and less variation than the sentences used in (Roesler and Nowé, 2019), the previous auxiliary word and phrase detection algorithms do not work.

Algorithm 1 The grounding procedure takes as input all words (W) and percepts (P) of the current situation, the sets of all previously obtained word-percept (WP) and percept-word (PW) pairs, the set of auxiliary words (AW), and the set of permanent phrases (PP) and returns the sets of grounded words (GW) and percepts (GP).

1: **procedure** GROUNDING(W, P, WP, PW, AW, PP)
2:     Substitute words with phrases from PP
3:     Update AW (Algorithm 2) and remove AW from W
4:     Update WP and PW using W and P
5:     **for** $j = 1$ to *word_number* **do**
6:         Save highest WP to GW
7:     **end for**
8:     **for** $j = 1$ to *percept_number* **do**
9:         Save highest PW to GP
10:     **end for**
11:     **return** $GW \cup GP$
12: **end procedure**

Thus, a novel auxiliary word detection algorithm (Algorithm 2) is proposed to handle the simpler sentences employed in this study[4], while no phrase detection is used to ensure a fair comparison with the baseline framework (Section 5), which does not have any phrase detection capabilities. The rest of this section provides an overview of the employed grounding algorithm.

For each situation all corresponding words and percepts are given to the grounding algorithm (Algorithm 1), while the sets of grounded words (GW) and percepts (GP) are initially empty. Before the actual grounding procedure, words that are part of known phrases will be combined so that they can be grounded together and auxiliary words are automatically detected and removed (Algorithm 2). Afterwards, all possible word-percept (WP) and percept-word (PW) pairs are created, i.e. for each word and percept a set containing all percepts and words they occurred with is created, and saved together with a number indicating how often the pair occurred. The highest word-percept pair is determined and saved to the set of grounded words (GW). All other word-percept pairs the word or

---

[3]The used DBSCAN implementation is available in *scikit-learn* (Pedregosa et al., 2011).

[4]Both auxiliary word mechanisms, i.e. the one used in (Roesler and Nowé, 2019) and the one proposed in this study, are used in parallel because both have shown to not produce false detections, i.e. they either detect an auxiliary word correctly or do not detect it.

Algorithm 2 The auxiliary word detection procedure takes as input the sets of word and percept occurrences (*WO* and *PO*), and the set of detected auxiliary words (AW).

1: **procedure** AUXILIARY WORD DETECTION(*WO*, *PO*, *AW*)
2:     **for** word, occurrence in *WO* **do**
3:         **if** $occurrence > max(PO) * 2$ **then**
4:             Add word to *AW*
5:         **end if**
6:     **end for**
7:     **return** *AW*
8: **end procedure**

---

percept are part of will no longer be considered for the selection of the highest word-percept pair in future iterations. This restriction is applied until all percepts have been used once for grounding. Afterwards, if some words have not been grounded, all percepts will become again available for grounding until all words have been grounded to allow grounding of synonyms. After all words have been grounded the same process is repeated for percept-word pairs to assign synonymous percepts to the same word. Finally, the sets of grounded words and percepts are merged.

5 Baseline Framework

The baseline framework consists of three parts: (1) 3D object segmentation component as described in Section (4.1), (2) Action recording component as described in Section (4.2), and (3) Bayesian learning model, which identifies auxiliary words and grounds non-auxiliary words and phrases through corresponding percepts. Since the perceptual data extraction components are the same for both frameworks, any difference in grounding performance can only be due to the different grounding algorithms, i.e. component three and four of the proposed framework (Sections 4.3 and 4.4) and component three of the baseline framework, which is described in the remainder of this section.

The probabilistic learning model, described in this section, is based on the model used in (Roesler et al., 2019), since the experimental setup employed in this study (Section 6) is also based on the scenario used in (Roesler et al., 2019). In general, the model has been chosen as a baseline because similar models have previously been em-

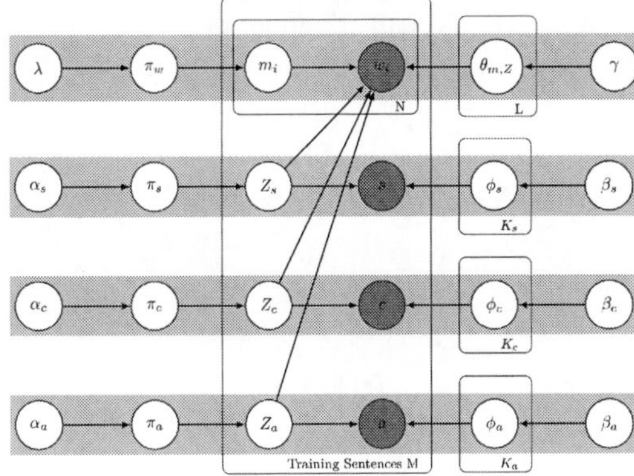

Figure 2: Graphical representation of the probabilistic model. Indices **i**, **s**, **c**, and **a** denote the order of words, object shapes, object colors, and actions, respectively.

Table 1: Definitions of the learning parameters in the graphical model.

Parameter	Definition
λ	Hyperparameter of the distribution π_w
$\alpha_s, \alpha_c, \alpha_a$	Hyperparameters of the distributions π_s, π_c and π_a
m_i	Modality index of each word (modality index $\in$ {Shape, Color, Action, AW})
Z_s, Z_c, Z_a	Indices of shape, color and action distributions
w_i	Word indices
s, c, a	Observed states representing shapes, colors and actions
γ	Hyperparameter of the distribution $\theta_{m,Z}$
$\beta_s, \beta_c, \beta_a$	Hyperparameters of the distributions ϕ_s, ϕ_c and ϕ_a
$\theta_{m,Z}$	Word distribution over modalities

ployed in similar grounding scenarios by different researchers, e.g. (Kollar et al., 2010; Tellex et al., 2011; Aly and Taniguchi, 2018; Roesler et al., 2018, 2019). In the model, the observed state w_i represents word indices, i.e. each individual word is represented by a different integer[5]. The observed state s represents the shape of objects, more specifically their geometric characteristics expressed through VFH descriptors (Section 4.1), c represents the color of objects and a represents actions. Table (1) provides a summary of the definitions of the learning model parameters. The corresponding probability distributions, i.e., w_i, $\theta_{m,Z_{L_1}}$, $\phi_{s_{K_1}}$, $\phi_{c_{K_2}}$, $\phi_{a_{K_3}}$, π_w, π_s, π_c, π_a, m_i, Z_s, Z_c, Z_a, s, c, and a, which characterize the different modalities in the graphical model, are defined in Equation (1), where *Cat* denotes a categorical distribution, *Dir* denotes a Dirichlet distribution, *GIW* denotes a Gaussian Inverse-Wishart distribution, and N denotes a mul-

---

[5]The following two example sentences illustrate the representation of words through word indices: (please, **1**) (lift up, **2**) (the, **3**) (brown, **4**) (coke, **5**) and (lift up, **2**) (the, **3**) (brownish, **6**) (lemonade, **7**), where the bold numbers indicate word indices.

tivariate Gaussian distribution.

$$
\begin{cases}
w_i & \sim & Cat(\theta_{m_i, Z_{m_i}}) \\
\theta_{m, Z_{L_1}} & \sim & Dir(\gamma) \quad, & L_1 = (1, ..., L) \\
\phi_{s K_1} & \sim & GIW(\beta_s), & K_1 = (1, ..., K_s) \\
\phi_{c K_2} & \sim & GIW(\beta_c), & K_2 = (1, ..., K_c) \\
\phi_{a K_3} & \sim & GIW(\beta_a), & K_3 = (1, ..., K_a) \\
\pi_w & \sim & Dir(\lambda) \\
\pi_s & \sim & Dir(\alpha_s) \\
\pi_c & \sim & Dir(\alpha_c) \\
\pi_a & \sim & Dir(\alpha_a) \\
m_i & \sim & Cat(\pi_w) \\
Z_s & \sim & Cat(\pi_s) \\
Z_c & \sim & Cat(\pi_c) \\
Z_a & \sim & Cat(\pi_a) \\
s & \sim & N(\phi_{Z_s}) \\
c & \sim & N(\phi_{Z_c}) \\
a & \sim & N(\phi_{Z_a})
\end{cases}
\tag{1}
$$

The latent variables of the Bayesian learning model are inferred using the Gibbs sampling algorithm (Geman and Geman, 1984) (Algorithm 3), which repeatedly samples from and updates the posterior distributions (Equation 2). Distributions were sampled for 100 iterations, after which convergence had been achieved.

$$
\begin{cases}
\phi_s & \sim & P(\phi_s | s, \beta_s) \\
\phi_c & \sim & P(\phi_c | c, \beta_c) \\
\phi_a & \sim & P(\phi_a | a, \beta_a) \\
\pi_w & \sim & P(\pi_w | \lambda, m) \\
\pi_s & \sim & P(\pi_s | \alpha_s, Z_s) \\
\pi_c & \sim & P(\pi_c | \alpha_c, Z_c) \\
\pi_a & \sim & P(\pi_a | \alpha_a, Z_a) \\
Z_s & \sim & P(Z_s | s, \pi_s, w) \\
Z_c & \sim & P(Z_c | c, \pi_c, w) \\
Z_a & \sim & P(Z_a | a, \pi_a, w) \\
\theta_{m, Z} & \sim & P(\theta_{m, Z} | m, Z_s, Z_c, Z_a, \gamma, w) \\
m_i & \sim & P(m_i | \theta_{m, Z}, Z_s, Z_c, Z_a, \pi_w, w_i)
\end{cases}
\tag{2}
$$

6 Experimental Setup

The experimental scenario used in this study is based on the scenario used in (Roesler et al., 2019). The main difference is the use of an additional modality, i.e. color, which leads to slightly different sentences. During the experiment a human tutor and HSR robot[6] interact in front

---

Algorithm 3 Inference of the model's latent variables. In this study, $nr\_of\_iterations$ was set to 100.

1: **procedure** GIBBS SAMPLING(W, P, WP, AW)
2:     Initialization of $\theta, \phi_s, \phi_c, \phi_a, \pi_w, \pi_s, \pi_c,$
3:     $\pi_a, Z_s, Z_c, Z_a, m_i$
4:     **for** $i = 1$ to $nr\_of\_iterations$ **do**
5:       Equation (2)
6:     **end for**
7:     **return** $\theta, \phi_s, \phi_c, \phi_a, \pi_w, \pi_s, \pi_c, \pi_a, Z_s,$
8:       Z_c, Z_a, m_i
9: **end procedure**

---

of a table, with one of the following five objects {BOTTLE, CUP, BOX, CAR, and BOOK} (Figure 1). Each interaction follows below procedure:

1. The human tutor places an object on the table and the robot determines the object's geometric characteristics and color to create corresponding feature vectors (Section 4.1).

2. An instruction, which describes how to manipulate the object, is given to the robot by the human tutor, e.g. "please lift up the red soda".

3. The human tutor teleoperates the robot to execute the action provided through the instruction while several kinematic characteristics are recorded and converted into an action feature vector (Section 4.2).

A total of 125 interactions were performed to record perceptual information for all combinations of employed shapes, colors, and actions. Since instruction words were selected randomly for each situation, except that words had to fit the encountered percepts, their number of occurrences in the data varies, e.g. the word "coffee" only occurs once, while the word "brown" occurs 14 times. Grounding was then performed for ten different interaction sequences, i.e. the order of the recorded situations was randomly changed, to ensure that the performance is not due to the specific order in which situations are encountered. Figure (3) shows how often each word occurred on average in all interactions as well as the training and test interactions.

---

[6]The Human Support Robot from Toyota, which is used for the experiment, has an omnidirectional movable cylindrical shaped body with one arm and gripper. It is equipped with a variety of different sensors, such as stereo and wide-angle cameras, and has 11 degrees of freedom.

Table 2: Overview of all percepts with their corresponding synonyms. The action percepts are explained in Table (3).

Type	Percept	Synonyms
Shape	Bottle	coca cola, soda, pepsi, coke, lemonade
	Cup	latte, milk, milk tea, coffee, espresso
	Box	candy, chocolate, confection, sweets, dark chocolate
	Car	audi, toyota, mercedes, bmw, honda
	Book	harry potter, narnia, lord of the rings, dracula, frankenstein
Color	Yellow	yellow, yellowish
	Pink	pink, pinkish
	Brown	brown, brownish
	Red	red, reddish
	White	white, whitish
Action	Lift up	lift up, raise
	Grab	grab, take
	Push	push, poke
	Pull	pull, drag
	Move	move, shift
Auxiliary Word	-	the
	-	please

Table 3: Explanations of the employed action percepts.

Percept	Description
Lift up	The object will be grabbed and lifted up.
Grab	The object will be grabbed, but not displaced.
Push	The object will be pushed with the closed gripper without being grabbed first.
Pull	The object will be grabbed and moved towards the robot.
Move	The object will be grabbed and moved away from the robot.

Each sentence consists of one of the following structures: "*action* the *color shape*" or "please *action* the *color shape*", where *action*, *color*, and *shape* are substituted by one of their corresponding words (Table 2). Each action and color can be referred to by two different words, while each shape has five corresponding words. During training and testing the obtained situations are given to the proposed and baseline frameworks. The former framework gets the situations separately one after the other, as if it is processing the data in real-time during the interaction. It first clusters the percepts of the current situation together with all previously encountered percepts to obtain abstract representations of shapes, colors and actions (Section 4.3). Afterwards, the CSL based grounding algorithm is used to ground words through the obtained cluster numbers (Section 4.4). In contrast, the baseline framework does not allow online learning and requires all sentences and corresponding percepts of the training situations to be given at once to the learning model.

7 Results and Discussion

The proposed cross-situational learning framework (Section 4) is evaluated through a human-robot interaction scenario (Section 6) and the obtained grounding results are compared to the groundings achieved by an unsupervised Bayesian grounding framework (Section 5). Figure (4) shows how

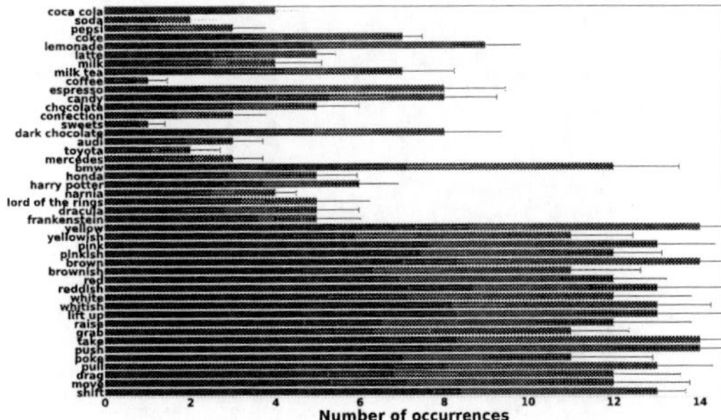

Figure 3: Word occurrences for all encountered words except auxiliary words. The dark blue part of the bars shows the mean number of occurrences during training and the bright blue part the mean number of occurrences during testing.

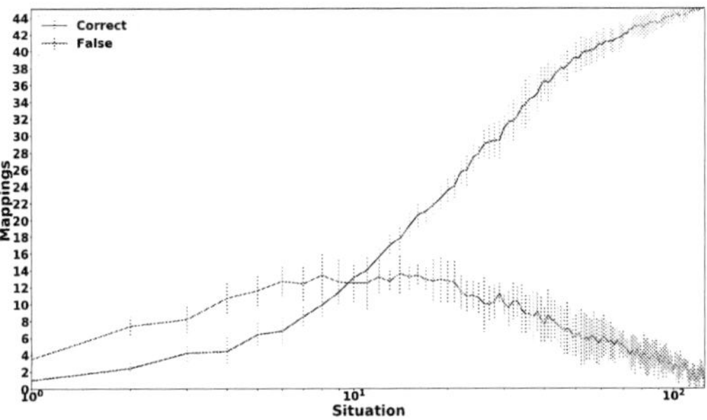

Figure 4: Mean number and standard deviation of correct and false mappings obtained by the proposed model over all 125 situations. The dotted part only occurs, when all situations are used for training, otherwise the model obtains only 43 correct mappings.

the mean number of correct and false mappings changes, when the proposed grounding framework encounters the employed situations one after the other. It also shows that all 45 correct mappings are obtained, when all 125 situations are used for training, while on average only 43 correct mappings are obtained, when only 60% of the situations are used for training. The figure also illustrates the online grounding capability of the model, i.e. that it updates its mappings with every new encountered situation, as well as its transparency because it allows to check at any time through which percept a word is grounded at that moment. Based on the collected co-occurrence information it would also be possible to calculate a confidence score for every mapping to understand how likely it is that a false mapping disappears or a correct mapping persists. The described transparency of the proposed framework can be helpful to understand and debug responses to instructions provided by a human,

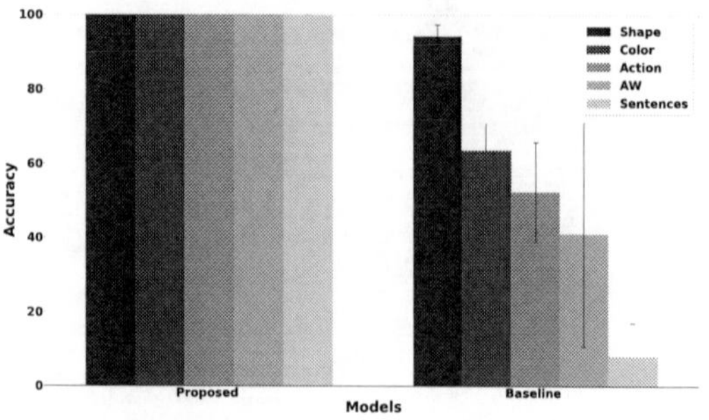

(a) All situations used for training and testing.

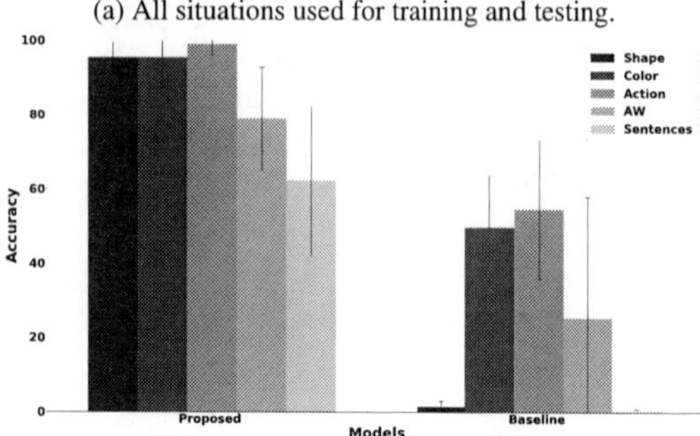

(b) 60% of the situations used for training and 40% for testing.

Figure 5: Mean grounding accuracy results and corresponding standard deviations for all modalities and both models. Additionally, the percentage of sentences for which all words were correctly grounded is shown.

when the framework is used to control an artifical agent interacting with a human, especially when the responses are incorrect or inappropriate.

In contrast, the baseline model requires an explicit training phase so that no corresponding figure, illustrating the number of correct and false mappings, can be created. Thus, to allow a comparison between the two models, the mappings of the proposed model are extracted after 125 and 75 situations, depending on the used train/test split. Two different train/test splits are analyzed in this study. For the first split, all situations are used for training and testing to see how well the frameworks perform when all test situations have been encountered before. For the second split, only 60% of the used situations are provided for training, while the remaining situations are used for testing. In this case, it is possible that some words never occur during training or only a limited number of times, e.g. once or twice. If a word does not occur during training, the proposed model is not able to obtain a corresponding mapping which leads to an accuracy of 0% as shown in Figure (6c) for the words *coffee* and *sweets*, which both only exist once in the dataset and are thus only present during train-

ing or testing, but not both. The word accuracies shown in Figure (6) were calculated by dividing the number of times a word was correctly grounded through the number of times the word was encountered during testing. Similar to the proposed model, the baseline model was also not able to ground the words *coffee* and *sweets* correctly, when only 60% of the situations were used for training. However, the baseline model also seems to require in general a higher minimum number of occurrences to successfully ground words, since there are many words that achieved a mean accuracy of 0%, when only 60% of the situations were used for training (Figure 6d).

Figure (5a) shows that the proposed model achieves perfect grounding, when the same situations are provided for training and testing, which confirms that it is able to obtain all correct mappings as shown in Figure (4). However, if only 60% of the situations are used for training and the remaining 40% unknown situations for testing the grounding accuracy drops for both models. For the proposed model the largest accuracy decrease is seen for auxiliary words, while still more than 95% of the obtained shape, color and action groundings are correct. For the baseline framework the largest drop in accuracy is seen for shapes, from more than 95% to less than 2%. The reason might be that every shape word has 5 synonyms, thus, if words would be equally distributed among all situations and specifically among the training and test sets, the decrease might not be as sharp. However, Figure 3 shows that the number of occurrences is not necessarily the reason for the drop because the words *bmw* and *narnia* occured on average 7 and 2.5 times during training, respectively, and *narnia* achieved an accuracy of about 5%, while the accuracy of *bmw* was 0% (Figure 6d). In contrast, the proposed model shows a more stable performance, since it was able to ground all non-auxiliary words that occured at least one time during training with a mean accuracy of more than 70%, while only the auxiliary word *please* achieved a lower mean accuracy of 30%.

Overall the evaluation shows that the proposed model outperforms the baseline model based on its auxiliary word detection and grounding accuracy. Interestingly, the performance difference is larger, when only 60% of the situations are used for training, although this scenario is artificially harming the proposed model by preventing it to learn during

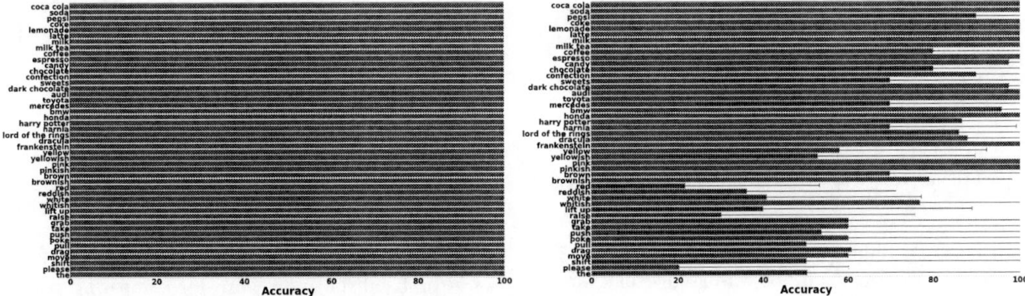

(a) Proposed model using all situations for training and testing. (b) Baseline model using all situations for training and testing.

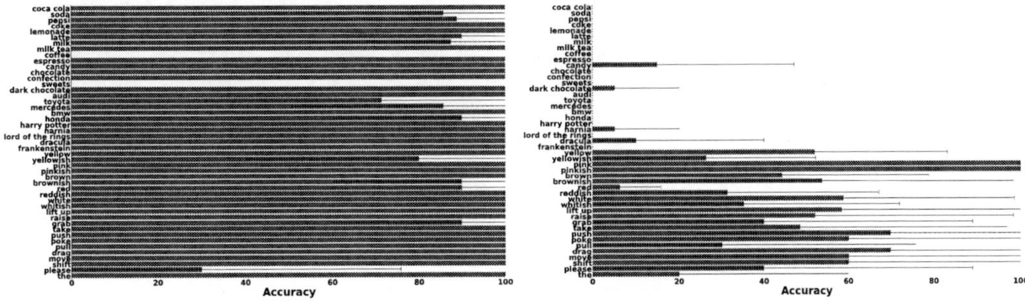

(c) Proposed model using 60% of the situations for training and (d) Baseline model using 60% of the situations for training and 40% for testing. 40% for testing.

Figure 6: Mean accuracy results and corresponding standard deviations for each individual word.

testing, since it does not require explicit training. In addition to the better grounding performance, the proposed model is also more transparent, which becomes important when robots are interacting with humans in complex and unrestricted environments, especially if some actions of the robots can cause harm to humans.

8 Conclusions and Future Work

This paper investigated a multimodal framework for grounding synonymous shape, color and action words through the visual perception and proprioception of a robot during its interaction with a human tutor. The cross-situational learning model was set up to learn the meaning of shape and color words of objects as well as action words using geometric characteristics and color information of objects obtained from point cloud information as well as kinematic features of the robot joints recorded during action execution.

The proposed model allowed auxiliary word detection and online grounding of synonyms through real percepts in an unsupervised manner and without the use of any syntactic or semantic information. Additionally, it outperformed the baseline model based on the accuracy of the obtained groundings,

its capability to process new situations online and its transparency.

In future work, different mechanisms will be investigated to improve the sample efficiency of the algorithm, which will become relevant, if a larger number of words is used or words occur less often. Additionally, it will be verified whether the framework can handle homonyms. Finally, supervised grounding methods will be integrated so that the robot is able to use human feedback, but does not require it.

References

N. Akhtar and L. Montague. 1999. Early lexical acquisition: the role of cross-situational learning. *First Language*, 19(57):347–358.

A. Aly and T. Taniguchi. 2018. Towards understanding object-directed actions: A generative model for grounding syntactic categories of speech through visual perception. In *IEEE International Conference on Robotics and Automation (ICRA)*, Brisbane, Australia.

R. A. Blythe, K. Smith, and A. D. M. Smith. 2010. Learning times for large lexicons through cross-situational learning. *Cognitive Science*, 34:620–642.

S. Carey. 1978. The child as word-learner. In M. Halle, J. Bresnan, and G. A. Miller, editors, *Linguistic theory and psychological reality*, pages 265–293. MIT Press, Cambridge, MA.

S. Carey and E. Bartlett. 1978. Acquiring a single new word. *Papers and Reports on Child Language Development*, 15:17–29.

C. Craye, D. Filliat, and J.-F. Goudou. 2016. Environment exploration for object-based visual saliency learning. In *IEEE International Conference on Robotics and Automation (ICRA)*, Stockholm, Sweden.

C. R. Dawson, J. Wright, A. Rebguns, M. V. Escárcega, D. Fried, and P. R. Cohen. 2013. A generative probabilistic framework for learning spatial language. In *IEEE Third Joint International Conference on Development and Learning and Epigenetic Robotics (ICDL)*, Osaka, Japan.

M. Ester, H.-P. Kriegel, J. Sander, and X. Xu. 1996. A density-based algorithm for discovering clusters in large spatial databases with noise. In *Proceedings of the 2nd International Conference on Knowledge Discovery and Data Mining (KDD)*, pages 226–231, Portland, Oregon, USA.

M. A. Fischler and R. C. Bolles. 1981. Random sample consensus: A paradigm for model fitting with applications to image analysis and automated cartography. *Communications of the ACM (CACM)*, 24(6):381–395.

C. Fisher, D. G. Hall, S. Rakowitz, and L. Gleitman. 1994. When it is better to receive than to give: Syntactic and conceptual constraints on vocabulary growth. *Lingua*, 92:333–375.

S. Geman and D. Geman. 1984. Stochastic relaxation, Gibbs distributions, and the Bayesian restoration of images. *IEEE Transactions on Pattern Analysis and Machine Intelligence (TPAMI)*, 6(6):721–741.

J. Gillette, H. Gleitman, L. Gleitman, and A. Lederer. 1999. Human simulations of vocabulary learning. *Cognition*, 73:135–176.

S. Harnad. 1990. The symbol grounding problem. *Physica D*, 42:335–346.

T. Kollar, S. Tellex, D. Roy, and N. Roy. 2010. Toward understanding natural language directions. In *Proceedings of the 5th ACM/IEEE International Conference on Human-Robot Interaction (HRI)*, Osaka, Japan.

F. Pedregosa, G. Varoquaux, A. Gramfort, V. Michel, B. Thirion, O. Grisel, M. Blondel, P. Prettenhofer, R. Weiss, V. Dubourg, J. Vanderplas, A. Passos, D. Cournapeau, M. Brucher, M. Perrot, and E. Duchesnay. 2011. Scikit-learn: Machine learning in python. *Journal of Machine Learning Research*, 12:2825–2830.

S. Pinker. 1989. *Learnability and cognition*. MIT Press, Cambridge, MA.

O. Roesler. 2019. A cross-situational learning based framework for grounding of synonyms in human-robot interactions. In *Proceedings of the Fourth Iberian Robotics Conference (ROBOT)*, Porto, Portugal.

O. Roesler, A. Aly, T. Taniguchi, and Y. Hayashi. 2018. A probabilistic framework for comparing syntactic and semantic grounding of synonyms through cross-situational learning. In *ICRA-18 Workshop on Representing a Complex World: Perception, Inference, and Learning for Joint Semantic, Geometric, and Physical Understanding.*, Brisbane, Australia.

O. Roesler, A. Aly, T. Taniguchi, and Y. Hayashi. 2019. Evaluation of word representations in grounding natural language instructions through computational human-robot interaction. In *Proceedings of the 14th ACM/IEEE International Conference on Human-Robot Interaction (HRI)*, Daegu, South Korea.

O. Roesler and A. Nowé. 2018. Simultaneous action learning and grounding through reinforcement and cross-situational learning. In *ALA 2018, Adaptive Learning Agents Workshop.*, Stockholm, Sweden.

O. Roesler and A. Nowé. 2019. Action learning and grounding in simulated human robot interactions. *The Knowledge Engineering Review*, 34(E13).

R. B. Rusu, G. Bradski, R. Thibaux, and J. Hsu. 2010. Fast 3D recognition and pose using the viewpoint feature histogram. In *Proceedings of the 2010 IEEE/RSJ International Conference on Intelligent Robots and Systems (IROS)*, pages 2155–2162, Taipei, Taiwan.

E. Schubert, J. Sander, M. Ester, H. P. Kriegel, and X. Xu. 2017. DBSCAN revisited, revisited: Why and how you should (still) use DBSCAN. *ACM Transactions on Database Systems (TODS)*, 42(3).

L. She, S. Yang, Y. Cheng, Y. Jia, J. Y. Chai, and N. Xi. 2014. Back to the blocks world: Learning new actions through situated human-robot dialogue. In *Proceedings of the SIGDIAL 2014 Conference*, pages 89–97, Philadelphia, U.S.A.

J. M. Siskind. 1996. A computational study of cross-situational techniques for learning word-to-meaning mappings. *Cognition*, 61:39–91.

A. D. M. Smith and K. Smith. 2012. *Cross-Situational Learning*, pages 864–866. Springer US, Boston, MA.

K. Smith, A. D. M. Smith, and R. A. Blythe. 2011. Cross-situational learning: An experimental study of word-learning mechanisms. *Cognitive Science*, 35(3):480–498.

L. Smith and C. Yu. 2008. Infants rapidly learn word-referent mappings via cross-situational statistics. *Cognition*, 106:1558–1568.

L. Steels and M. Loetzsch. 2012. The grounded naming game. In L. Steels, editor, *Experiments in Cultural Language Evolution*, pages 41–59. John Benjamins, Amsterdam.

S. Tellex, T. Kollar, S. Dickerson, M. R. Walter, A. G. Banerjee, S. Teller, and N. Roy. 2011. Approaching the symbol grounding problem with probabilistic graphical models. *AI Magazine*, 32(4):6476.

Toyota Motor Corporation. 2017. *HSR Manual*, 2017.4.17 edition.

P. Vogt. 2012. Exploring the robustness of cross-situational learning under zipfian distributions. *Cognitive Science*, 36(4):726–739.

Leveraging Multimodal Behavioral Analytics for Automated Job Interview Performance Assessment and Feedback

Anumeha Agrawal *, Rosa Anil George *, Selvan Sunitha Ravi *, Sowmya Kamath S and
Anand Kumar M
Department of Information Technology
National Institute of Technology Karnataka, Surathkal, India 575025
{anumehaagrawal29, rosageorge97, sunitha98selvan}@gmail.com,
{sowmyakamath, m_anandkumar}@nitk.edu.in

Abstract

Behavioral cues play a significant part in human communication and cognitive perception. In most professional domains, employee recruitment policies are framed such that both professional skills and personality traits are adequately assessed. Hiring interviews are structured to evaluate expansively a potential employee's suitability for the position - their professional qualifications, interpersonal skills, ability to perform in critical and stressful situations, in the presence of time and resource constraints, etc. Therefore, candidates need to be aware of their positive and negative attributes and be mindful of behavioral cues that might have adverse effects on their success. We propose a multimodal analytical framework that analyzes the candidate in an interview scenario and provides feedback for predefined labels such as engagement, speaking rate, eye contact, etc. We perform a comprehensive analysis that includes the interviewee's facial expressions, speech, and prosodic information, using the video, audio, and text transcripts obtained from the recorded interview. We use these multimodal data sources to construct a composite representation, which is used for training machine learning classifiers to predict the class labels. Such analysis is then used to provide constructive feedback to the interviewee for their behavioral cues and body language. Experimental validation showed that the proposed methodology achieved promising results.

Keywords: Behavioral analysis, Multimodal Analytics, Personality computing

1 Introduction

In the business world, interviews are a prerequisite to personnel recruitment for assessing the candidates through a structured interaction and discussion either on a one-to-one basis or by a panel of interviewers. It is an opportunity for the candidates to prove that they are qualified for the position, and for recruiters to assess the job-to-candidate fit. Such recruiters are trained in evaluating a candidate's personality, thought patterns, behavior under stressful situations, and emotional intelligence through well-established metrics through technical analysis, psychometric testing, etc. Several theoretical models (Goldberg et al., 1981) have suggested the "big five trait taxonomy", based on which an individual's traits can be summarized, and scoring can be performed for choosing a candidate (John et al., 1999).

The field of personality computing focuses on automatically analyzing such essential insights into the psyche of a person based on their behavior, verbal responses and non-verbal actions, speech patterns, body language, etc (Vinciarelli and Mohammadi, 2014). Studies have shown that nonverbal behaviors such as smiling, maintaining eye contact, and good posture all contribute significantly to interpersonal communication along with an indication as to the mental health and well-being of the participants (Krishnan and Kamath, 2019). The significant difference between verbal and non-verbal communication is that the former is specific and interpreted, while the latter is subtle and implied. Both channels of communication affect conversational dynamics and influence the relationship between individuals (Somant and Madan, 2015).

Automating such behavioral analysis can be beneficial while conducting mass recruitment drives, primarily when many of these are done online through videoconferencing systems. From the candidates' perspective, knowing the effect of their own verbal and non-verbal behavior in creating a favorable impression and increasing their chances of success in interviews is also of significant interest. These cues may be available through their

---

*equal contribution

Proceedings of the 58th Annual Meeting of the Association for Computational Linguistics, pages 46–54
Seattle, USA, July5 - 10, 2020. ©2017 Association for Computational Linguistics
https://doi.org/10.18653/v1/P17

interview videos and audio, speaking qualities, and the effect of content delivery. Analysis of a single modality can often be insufficient in obtaining usable insights into how humans perceive and express information (Agrawal et al., 2019). Modalities other than text can commonly present clues for the expression of sentiment and feelings (Ding and Ding, 2013). Audio and visual features also aid in linguistic disambiguation as they provide additional details regarding the speakers' sentiment. When a person speaks with optimal vocal modulation or using appropriate gestures, it conveys a lot more than just the content.

Research on automated analysis of both verbal and non-verbal behavior cues in the case of job interviews has recently gained momentum, which we aim to analyze in this work. In this paper, we experiment with several linguistic, audio, and visual features extracted from recorded interviews to create feature vectors passed to different classifiers to score the candidate on specific predefined labels. The remainder of this paper is organized as follows: Section 2 presents a discussion on existing works in the area of interest. The details of the proposed methodology and specifics of implementation are presented in Section 3. In Section 4, the experimental analysis and performance of the various models for each task are discussed, followed by the conclusion and references.

2   Related work

Over the last decade, behavioral patterns analysis using multimodal data has received significant research attention. Navas et al. (2006) conducted experiments for speech-based emotion analysis to compare speaker-dependent and speaker-independent techniques. To perform this analysis, several acoustic features such as fundamental frequency, duration, intensity are extracted to find hidden information. However, the speaker-dependent approach was not scalable and cannot be used in large-scale applications with several users. Borth et al. (2013) proposed a different approach for sentiment analysis of visual content using SentiBank. SentiBank is a visual concept detector library used to extract various concepts and Adjective Noun Pairs (ANP) from the visual content. While existing models predicted sentiments or emotions directly from low-level visual features, their approach used high-level visual features to better capture sentiments. They use images to extract mid-level

semantic features and use a classifier to predict semantic features, which can be used to determine the relevance and importance of the image in determining emotion.

Nguyen et al. (2013) used real-time interview data to monitor and analyze body communication cues. The interviewees are seated in the videos, which lets them analyze both upper body movement and facial cues. Various visual features are automatically extracted, and data is annotated to predict the personality and job interview ratings. This model shows the importance of using bodily gestures to predict the personality and give interview ratings. Naim et al. (2015) collated and used the MIT Interview dataset and trained Lasso and SVR models to predict several emotions and verbal/nonverbal cues like EyeContact, Calm, Speaking Rate, Authentic, Focused, Structured Answers, Smiled, Friendly, Engagement, etc. These labeled ratings were manually assigned by Amazon Turk Workers, and the ground truth labels were derived by averaging the scores of 9 Turk workers.

Pereira et al. (2016) presented a new technique for sentiment analysis in the telecommunication domain. They extracted and combined prosodic, lexical, and visual features from news videos and applied various computational methods to recognize real-time emotions from facial cues. The speech delivered by each participant is processed, parsed, and sentiment analysis is done on the corresponding text transcript. Features such as visual power of perceived emotion, field sizes of members, voicing likelihood, sound intensity, the fundamental frequency of the speech, and the scores associated with the sentiment were defined and used. One of the limitations is that the poor audio quality of the chosen dataset resulted in inaccurate sentiment prediction. Another drawback observed is due to the selected distance metric, the model does not map well to the intensity of the sentiment.

In recent years, behavioral pattern analysis using multimodal data has received significant research attention. The rise in online video streaming and hosting websites such as YouTube has facilitated an increase in sentiment expressions in multiple modalities (Pravalika et al., 2017). The availability of standard datasets containing videos annotated for emotion or sentiment has also has been conducive to this, as shown in (Zadeh et al., 2016).

Chen et al. (2016) generated a multimodal corpus with structured interview responses, by manually rating the interviewee's personality and performance for 12 structured interview questions which measure different types of job related skills. Along with interviews, the interviewee's public speaking videos were also recorded and used to provide useful cues. They used visual, lexical and speech features, based on which they showed that using both non-verbal and verbal cues outperforms other cases. Poria et al. (2017) studied the emotions from facial expressions, reporting that standard facial expressions are sufficient to provide several clues to detect emotions. Speech-based emotion analysis based on the identification of various acoustic features, such as the intensity of utterance, bandwidth, pitch, and duration, is also helpful. They achieved a 5-10% improvement in performance compared, however, the contextual relationship between utterances are considered and treated equally in this model. Cambria et al. (2017)'s multimodal emotion recognition model extracts features from text and videos using a convolutional neural network architecture, incorporating all three modalities- visual, audio, and text. Radhakrishnan et al. (2018) proposed a new approach for sentiment analysis from audio clips, which uses a hybrid of the Keyword Spotting System. The Maximum Entropy classifier was designed to integrate audio and text processing into a single system, and this model outperformed other conventional classifiers.

Blanchard et al. (2018) developed a fusion technique for audio and video modalities using audio and video features to analyze spoken sentences for the sentiment. They did not consider the traditional transcription features to minimize human intervention. However, the model can be scaled and deployed in the real world effortlessly. They selected high dimensional features for the model to test their generalizability in the sentiment detection domain. Hu and Flaxman (2018) presented a novel approach that uses deep learning to identify the sentiment of multimodal data. The modalities considered were images and text, and computer vision techniques were combined with text mining. Their aim was to treat it as a study of emotion, one of the most exciting fields in psychology. They did this using a large social media dataset of Tumblr posts, using which the emotion word tags attached by users was predicted, treating these as emotions reported by the user. Their work combined image and text and proved that combining these two modalities conveyed more information about the

sentiment that either of the modalities alone.

Based on the review of existing work, several limitations were observed. When features from different modalities are considered, it is crucial to find only those features that influence the label. Thus, we aim to address the issue of feature selection by experimenting with different feature selection algorithms. Many features are strongly correlated to each other, and considering these strongly correlated features together will not add a lot of value in predicting a label. Identifying and removing such features that are strongly correlated to each other and considering only one such feature in predicting the label can be more beneficial.

3 Proposed Approach

In this section, the proposed model and its associated processes are described in detail. Our approach is built on all three modalities, and the data modality-specific preprocessing techniques and various algorithms used to classify the data for each of the labels, are presented. For experimental validation, we used the MIT interview dataset (Naim et al., 2015), which consists of recordings of 138 mock job interviews of 69 candidates pre-intervention and post-intervention. It contains Amazon Mechanical Turk Worker scores for each video, which when averaged gives the final score for each of the labels. It includes the audio files as well, which we use for audio analysis. In contrast to Naim et al. (2015) who used regression as their evaluation metric, we use classification, with the numbers 1 to 7 representing the level of performance. A score of 1 for any label is treated as very bad performance whereas a score of 7 is treated as exceptionally good. We use class labels as, our objective is to provide users with feedback based on the class label.

3.1 Prosodic Features

Prosodic features play an essential role in characterizing the speaking style of the interviewee. Frequency, pitch information, tone, intensity, spectral energy, spectral centroid, zero-crossing rate, etc. are some of the prosodic features which are considered to be primary in analyzing the speaking style and emotions. In (Naim et al., 2015), the pitch information, vocal intensities, characteristics of the first three formants, and spectral energy were included. We found that time-domain features are of utmost importance as the emotion can be predicted by considering several frames together. We used the raw audio signals to extract the time domain features. Using the magnitude of the Discrete Fourier Transform (DFT), we calculated the frequency domain features. The cepstral domain is computed using the Inverse DFT on the logarithmic spectrum. These features can be extracted for windows of small and large sizes. In our methodology, we used a short term window and split the audio signal into short-term windows (frames). We extracted features for each frame, giving us a feature vector of 40 elements, using a short term window size between 20ms and 100ms. The pyAudioAnalysis (Giannakopoulos, 2015) library of Python was used to generate the features for the audio. Other frameworks, such as PRAAT (Boersma and Weenink, 2018), can also be used to extract prosodic features.

3.2 Facial Expressions

Landmarks are to be first captured for extracting facial features, which are essential points of interest on a person's face. The global transformations, including rotation, translation, and scaling were disregarded, and only the local changes were considered while extracting features from the tracked interest points. These local changes can provide useful information about our facial expressions. OpenCV was used to extract each landmark, namely, nose, left mouth, right mouth, chin, left eye left corner, and right eye right corner from each frame. The video was broken down into frames of size 1 second, and features are extracted. These were averaged over the given time frame of the video. We also incorporated the head pose features (Pitch, Roll, and Yaw) based on the corresponding elements of the rotation matrix R. A pre-trained convolutional neural network called LeNet (LeCun et al., 1998), consisting of two alternate Conv layers, a pooling layer, and finally, a fully connected layer was used for detecting a person smiling or not was used. LeNet was trained on the SMILES dataset (Arigbabu et al., 2016) consisting of 13,165 face images, of dimension 64x64x1 (grayscale).

3.3 Lexical Features

The linguistic features provide insightful information regarding the confidence and the style of speech of the interview candidate. The most commonly used feature for text is the counts of individual unique words. It gives a clear understanding of proficiency, eloquence, and the ability to use proper vocabulary during a structured communication episode like an interview.

To obtain lexical features, the text transcripts of all the audio clips were obtained, using the Google Cloud Speech-to-Text API. Once we obtain all the text transcripts, text cleaning was done before further processing. All letters were converted to lowercase, after which punctuation marks, accent marks, and any extra white spaces were removed. Tokenization was performed to split the text into smaller units, using the Natural Language Toolkit (Bird et al., 2008), a Python library for tokenization. Next, the speaking style features were extracted, like the average number of words spoken per minute, the average number of unique words per minute, count of unique words in the transcript, and the number of filler words used per minute. Information regarding speaking rate, proficiency, and fluency of a particular candidate can be evaluated using these features. Pereira et al. (2016) computed the sentiment score for each sentence in the closed captions as a summation over the generated vector assigning the sentiment (-1,0,1) for each method. We incorporated a similar logic to obtain the emotion scores.

Finally, to get a detailed analysis of the overall emotion of the text, we used the Tone Analyzer (Akkiraju, 2015). Each sentence is passed through the Tone Analyzer, and the percentage of emotion in that sentence in the following categories- Joy, Sadness, Tentative, Analytical, Fear, and Anger, is calculated. Each interview is assigned the average score per category, as mentioned earlier. The Stanford Named Entity Recognizer (NER) (Finkel et al., 2005) was also used to obtain the count of nouns, adjectives, and verbs in each sentence.

3.4 Class Prediction

Several experiments were carried out after and before the feature selection process. Each of these experiments was carried out for individual labels, and we made several interesting observations. We experimented with four machine learning algorithms - Random Forest, Support Vector Machine Classifier (SVC), Multitask Lasso Model, and Multilayer Perceptron (MLP).

Random Forest (Breiman, 2001) build decision trees on data samples that get chosen randomly. A prediction is obtained from each decision tree, and the most optimal solution is selected through voting. We used attribute selection techniques such as Information gain, Gini index, and Gain ratio to generate each decision tree and obtain the final voting. With this model, the issue of overfitting is avoided as the biases get canceled out by taking an average of the predictions. Support Vector Classifiers (Cortes and Vapnik, 1995) find an appropriate hyperplane in an N-dimensional space to classify the data points distinctly. The support vector classifier aims to maximize the margin between the hyperplane and data points. The Multi-task Lasso model (Lozano and Swirszcz, 2012) penalizes least-squares along with regularization to suppress or shrink features. The Lasso makes use of both feature selection and continuous shrinkage due to the nature of the norm penalty. The optimization objective for Lasso can be calculated using Eq. (1) and Eq. (2), where n represents the sample size considered, Y is the vector containing the target values, X is the training data, W denotes the weight matrix, α is a constant that is multiplied with the L1-norm of the coefficient vector.

$$1/(2 * n_{samples})) * ||Y - XW||^2 + \alpha ||W||_{21} \quad (1)$$

where,

$$||W||_{21} = \sum_i \sqrt{\sum_j w_{ij}^2} \quad (2)$$

The Multi-layer Perceptron (MLP) is a supervised learning algorithm that helps the target learn a non-linear function approximator, given a set of features. There may exist one or may non-linear layers known as hidden layers between the first (input) and last (output) layers. A single hidden layer makes the model a universal approximator, while also supporting multi-label classification and learning non-linear models.

3.5 Implementation

The features generated from the three different modalities - text, audio, and video were used to construct a feature vector, which is then passed through various classifiers to predict the class for the labels. As discussed, four different algorithms - Random Forest, SVC, Multitask Lasso, and MLP were used as classifiers. The features used to build the feature vector were:

1. *Audio* - Power, intensity, duration, pitch, zero-crossing rate, energy, the entropy of energy, spectral centroid, spectral flux, spectral spread, spectral roll-off, MFCCs, Chroma vector, Chroma deviation.

2. *Video* - Nose, chin, left eye left corner, right eye right corner, left mouth, right mouth landmarks, yaw, pitch, roll, smiling or not smiling.

3. *Lexical* - speaking rate, proficiency, fluency, count of total words spoken, Count of total unique words spoken, the emotion of the text, the score associated with the emotion, count of Nouns, Verbs, Adjectives.

Once the fused feature vector is obtained, the ML classifiers are trained to predict the ratings of the interview on a scale of 1-7 based on 9 different parameters - Eye Contact, Speaking rate, Engaged, Pauses, Calmness, Not stressed, Focused, Authentic and Not Awkward. These parameters are influenced by a set of selected features from the feature vector, as processed from the dataset. Thus, we take different combinations of lexical, prosody, and facial features to find the optimal features for each of the parameters. Feature selection techniques are also employed for obtaining the optimal feature vector. The data is first normalized using standardization and scaled to unit variance. The standard score of sample x is calculated using the Eq. (3), where u is the mean of the training samples, and s is the standard deviation of the training samples.

$$z = (x - u)/s \quad (3)$$

Each feature is centered and scaled based on the mean computed for the samples in the training set. Automatic feature selection is carried out to eliminate redundant and irrelevant features. Different feature selection processes are performed for each of the parameters. During K best feature selection, a correlation matrix is calculated, and k features that have the highest scores indicating strong relationships with the output variable are retained, while the other features are eliminated.

Based on the feature vector selected, we also experimented to find the optimal value of k as well. We used the Benjamini-Hochberg procedure (Thissen et al., 2002) to decrease the false discovery rate, as it helps control the influence of small p-values, which often leads to rejection of a true null hypothesis. Due to this, the number of false positives is mostly decreased. For this, the p values for all variables are calculated and then ranked. The variables with p values higher than a threshold value are retained, while all other variables are eliminated. Family-based errors are used to calculate the probability of false positives so that features that cause Type I errors can be eliminated.

During our experiments, we found that several features were correlated with each other. In such cases, just one of the features can be retained, and the rest can be ignored. Through several experiments, we determined the ideal threshold value for correlation, as 0.6. The ML models were then trained to predict ratings for each of the label parameters. We try different combinations of feature selection methods and algorithms and observed their effect on the performance. This helped in understanding the most well-suited model for different settings. For each algorithm, an extensive search is performed over specified hyper-parameter values to help ensure that the models do not perform poorly due to a lack of hyperparameter tuning. We used 3 fold cross-validation to ensure that our models perform well in the real world as well.

4   Experimental Results and Analysis

For extensively evaluating the proposed multimodal analytics pipeline, various combinations of prosodic, visual, and lexical features were experimented with, and used to train the four different classifiers, discussed in Section 3. each classifier is trained to predict from 9 different class labels - *eye contact, speaking rate, engaged, pauses, calmness, not stresses, focused, authentic, and not awkward.* Experiments using the fused multimodal feature vector were performed, the results of which are tabulated in Table 1. As can be observed from Table 1, the Random Forest Classifier outperformed the others for the *Eye Contact* class, with an accuracy of 64.28% obtained when the family-wise error technique of feature selection was used (further experiments were conducted to evaluate the effect of different modalities, this is presented in Table 2). Most models were able to predict a rating for *Speaking rate* with high accuracy of 96.43%. The Lasso

Classifier with Benjamini-Hochberg technique and Random Forest Classifier with the family-wise error technique helped achieve the best results. For the *Engaged* label, an accuracy of 75% using the Support Vector Classifier, along with the family-wise error technique of feature selection was obtained, while for *Pauses*, an accuracy of 82.14% using the Random Forest Classifier and the K best feature selection was seen as the best.

Two models performed well on the dataset to achieve an accuracy of 78.57% on the *Calmness* parameter - the Support Vector Classifier with the Benjamini-Hochberg technique and the Random Forest Classifier with K best feature selection technique. The Random Forest Classifier and Support Vector Classifier achieved an accuracy of 82.14% for *Not Stressed* label, while the Random Forest Classifier with the family-wise error technique outperformed other variations for the *Focused* label. For the *Authentic* label, the best accuracy obtained was only 67.87% using the Random Forest Classifier with the family-wise error technique of feature selection when Lexical and Facial features were used. For the *Not Awkward* label, the Random Forest Classifier showed the best performance at 60.71%, though still low when compared to other class labels. Random Forest performed the best for 8 out of 9 labels. This is because it selects features that contribute the most to the classification as it considers the average of all predictions, canceling out the bias. However, MLP underperformed on most of the parameters.

Another objective was to check how the different modalities measure up when feature sets using any two modalities are created and ML models are trained using these features. This basically provides insights into which modalities provide an edge in capturing personality-specific traits. To as-

Table 1: Best accuracy scores obtained for models trained on audio+video+lexical multimodal feature vector

Label	Random Forest	SVC	Multitask Lasso	MLP
Eye contact	0.5714	0.5714	0.5714	0.5714
Speaking rate	0.9643	0.8928	0.9642	0.7857
Engaged	0.6428	0.7500	0.6428	0.5383
Pauses	0.8214	0.7857	0.6785	0.6785
Calmness	0.7857	0.7857	0.7500	0.6071
Not Stressed	0.8214	0.8214	0.6785	0.7500
Focused	0.7500	0.7142	0.7142	0.7142
Authentic	0.6787	0.6428	0.4642	0.6428
Not Awkward	0.6071	0.464	0.4285	0.45357

Table 2: Observed accuracy scores for different combinations of modalities using a Random Forest Classifier.

Label	Audio+Video+Lexical	Audio+Video	Lexical+Video	Audio+Lexical
Eye Contact	0.5714	0.6428	0.5714	0.5428
Speaking rate	0.9643	0.9285	0.9285	0.9285
Engaged	0.6428	0.6428	0.6071	0.6071
Pauses	0.8214	0.7857	0.7857	0.7857
Calmness	0.7857	0.7500	0.7500	0.7857
Not Stressed	0.8214	0.7500	0.7142	0.8214
Focused	0.7500	0.5714	0.6071	0.6071
Authentic	0.6787	0.6071	0.6785	0.6428
Not Awkward	0.6071	0.4285	0.2500	0.4285

Table 3: Observed accuracy scores for individual modalities using Random Forest Classifier

Label	Audio	Video	Lexical
Eye Contact	0.5000	0.6071	0.4642
Speaking rate	0.8571	0.8571	0.8571
Engaged	0.5357	0.4642	0.5357
Pauses	0.6071	0.6071	0.6428
Calmness	0.6785	0.6785	0.6785
Not stressed	0.7500	0.7142	0.7857
Focused	0.7857	0.7142	0.6785
Authentic	0.4642	0.5357	0.5714
Not Awkward	0.5000	0.2857	0.2142

Table 4: Best accuracy scores for different feature selection techniques.

Label	Benjamini-Hochberg	Family-wise error selection	K best feature selection
Eye Contact	0.5714	0.6428	0.5714
Speaking rate	0.9643	0.9643	0.9285
Engaged	0.6428	0.7500	0.6071
Pauses	0.7124	0.7857	0.8214
Calmness	0.7857	0.7500	0.7857
Not Stressed	0.7142	0.8214	0.7857
Focused	0.6875	0.7500	0.6071
Authentic	0.5357	0.6787	0.6428
Not Awkward	0.6071	0.5714	0.5357

sess this behaviour, we conducted experiments with three combinations of modalities - *Audio+video*, *Lexical+video* and *Audio+lexical* as well as experimented with individual modalities. The random forest classifier was trained on feature sets generated by fusing these modalities to create three different two-modality feature sets, after which the label prediction performance was then observed. Similarly, we also considered each of the three modalities on their own, that is, the audio, video and lexical feature sets. Again, the best performing classifier, Random Forest was trained separately on the one-modality feature vectors, and label prediction performance was observed.

Table 2 and Table 3 show the results obtained from two-modality feature vectors and each individual modality feature vector for the best performing classifier, Random Forest, respectively. We observed that the performance varies significantly when the classifiers are trained on different combinations of the modality-specific feature set. For the *Eye contact* class, the *Audio+video+lexical* feature vector was not very accurate. In fact, the two-modality feature vector performed better than the three-modality feature vector. However, for all other classes, the Random Forest classifier trained on the three-modality feature vector outperformed all other variants. Table 4 shows the accuracy scores for the different feature selection techniques when all the modalities are considered.

5 Concluding Remarks

In this paper, approaches to automatically assess candidates' strengths and weaknesses during an interview, using the video, audio, and transcripts of the interview was presented. Various preprocessing steps, including normalization and feature extraction for each of the three modalities was performed, followed by feature selection to select the best features from each modality. Label classification was performed using four machine learning models - Random Forest, Support Vector Classifier, Multitask Lasso, and Multi-Layer Perceptron model on the optimal set of fused features and their variations. Effect of various combinations of modalities and feature selection techniques are experimented with. The models were trained for prediction with respect to nine labels to evaluate the candidate. Experiments revealed that the Random Forest Classifier outperformed all other models for 8 out of the 9 labels considered.

The current dataset has only 169 videos, making it difficult to get a very high accuracy for all the labels. The dataset could be expanded to include more interview videos that are scored by Amazon Turk workers. We also aim to improve the predictions by incorporating behaviors such as hand movements and body posture to get a refined understanding of the candidate's performance. The current model will be integrated into a web application that can be used as a feedback tool to train candidates for interviews by providing them with real-time feedback on their performance and pointers to manage their strengths and weaknesses. The scores can then be interpreted to give meaningful suggestions to the candidate for boosting their interview performance.

References

Anumeha Agrawal, Rosa Anil George, Selvan Sunitha Ravi, Sowmya Kamath, and Anand Kumar. 2019. ARS_NITK at MEDIQA 2019: Analysing various methods for natural language inference, recognising question entailment and medical question answering system. In *Proceedings of the 18th BioNLP Workshop and Shared Task, ACL 2019*, pages 533–540.

Rama Akkiraju. 2015. Ibm watson tone analyzer—new service now available. *IBM Cloud Blog, Jul,* 16.

Olasimbo Ayodeji Arigbabu, Saif Mahmood, Sharifah Mumtazah Syed Ahmad, and Abayomi A Arigbabu. 2016. Smile detection using hybrid face representation. *Journal of Ambient Intelligence and Humanized Computing*, 7(3):415–426.

Steven Bird, Ewan Klein, and Edward Loper. 2008. Nltk documentation. *Online: accessed April.*

Nathaniel Blanchard, Daniel Moreira, Aparna Bharati, and Walter J Scheirer. 2018. Getting the subtext without the text: Scalable multimodal sentiment classification from visual and acoustic modalities. *arXiv preprint arXiv:1807.01122.*

Paul Boersma and David Weenink. 2018. Praat: Doing phonetics by computer [computer program]. version 6.0. 37. *RetrievedFebruary*, 3:2018.

Damian Borth, Rongrong Ji, Tao Chen, Thomas Breuel, and Shih-Fu Chang. 2013. Large-scale visual sentiment ontology and detectors using adjective noun pairs. In *Proceedings of the 21st ACM International Conference on Multimedia*, MM '13, pages 223–232, New York, NY, USA. ACM.

Leo Breiman. 2001. Random forests. *Mach. Learn.,* 45(1):5–32.

Erik Cambria, Devamanyu Hazarika, Soujanya Poria, Amir Hussain, and RBV Subramanyam. 2017. Benchmarking multimodal sentiment analysis. In *International Conference on Computational Linguistics and Intelligent Text Processing*, pages 166–179. Springer.

Lei Chen, Gary Feng, Michelle Martin-Raugh, Chee Wee Leong, Christopher Kitchen, Su-Youn Yoon, Blair Lehman, Harrison Kell, and Chong Min Lee. 2016. Automatic scoring of monologue video interviews using multimodal cues. In *INTERSPEECH*, pages 32–36.

Corinna Cortes and Vladimir Vapnik. 1995. Support-vector networks. *Mach. Learn.*, 20(3):273–297.

Huiling Ding and Xin Ding. 2013. 360-degree rhetorical analysis of job hunting: A four-part, multimodal project. *Business Communication Quarterly*, 76(2):239–248.

Jenny Rose Finkel, Trond Grenager, and Christopher Manning. 2005. Incorporating non-local information into information extraction systems by gibbs sampling. In *Proceedings of the 43rd annual meeting on association for computational linguistics*, pages 363–370. Association for Computational Linguistics.

Theodoros Giannakopoulos. 2015. pyaudioanalysis: An open-source python library for audio signal analysis. *PloS one*, 10(12).

LS Goldberg, LH Goldberg, LR GOLDBERG, LR Goldberg, L Goldberg, and R Goldberg. 1981. Language and individual differences: The search for universals in personality lexicons.

Anthony Hu and Seth Flaxman. 2018. Multimodal sentiment analysis to explore the structure of emotions. In *Proceedings of the 24th ACM SIGKDD International Conference on Knowledge Discovery & Data Mining*, KDD '18, pages 350–358, New York, NY, USA. ACM.

Oliver P John, Sanjay Srivastava, et al. 1999. The big five trait taxonomy: History, measurement, and theoretical perspectives. *Handbook of personality: Theory and research*, 2(1999):102–138.

Gokul S Krishnan and Sowmya S Kamath. 2019. A novel ga-elm model for patient-specific mortality prediction over large-scale lab event data. *Applied Soft Computing*, 80:525–533.

Yann LeCun, Léon Bottou, Yoshua Bengio, and Patrick Haffner. 1998. Gradient-based learning applied to document recognition. *Proceedings of the IEEE*, 86(11):2278–2324.

Aurélie C. Lozano and Grzegorz Swirszcz. 2012. Multi-level lasso for sparse multi-task regression. In *Proceedings of the 29th International Coference on International Conference on Machine Learning*, ICML'12, page 595–602, Madison, WI, USA. Omnipress.

Iftekhar Naim, M Iftekhar Tanveer, Daniel Gildea, and Mohammed Ehsan Hoque. 2015. Automated prediction and analysis of job interview performance: The role of what you say and how you say it. In *2015 11th IEEE International Conference and Workshops on Automatic Face and Gesture Recognition (FG)*, volume 1, pages 1–6. IEEE.

Eva Navas, Inma Hernáez, and Iker Luengo. 2006. An objective and subjective study of the role of semantics and prosodic features in building corpora for emotional tts. *IEEE transactions on audio, speech, and language processing*, 14(4):1117–1127.

Laurent Son Nguyen, Alvaro Marcos-Ramiro, Martha Marrón Romera, and Daniel Gatica-Perez. 2013. Multimodal analysis of body communication cues in employment interviews. In *Proceedings of the 15th ACM on International conference on multimodal interaction*, pages 437–444.

Moisés Henrique Ramos Pereira, Flávio Luis Cardeal Pádua, Adriano César Machado Pereira, Fabrício Benevenuto, and Daniel Hasan Dalip. 2016. Fusing audio, textual, and visual features for sentiment analysis of news videos. In *Tenth International AAAI Conference on Web and Social Media*.

Soujanya Poria, Erik Cambria, Devamanyu Hazarika, Navonil Majumder, Amir Zadeh, and Louis-Philippe Morency. 2017. Context-dependent sentiment analysis in user-generated videos. In *Proceedings of the 55th Annual Meeting of the Association for Computational Linguistics (Volume 1: Long Papers)*, pages 873–883.

A Pravalika, Vishvesh Oza, NP Meghana, and Sowmya Kamath. 2017. Domain-specific sentiment analysis approaches for code-mixed social network data. In *2017 8th international conference on computing, communication and networking technologies (ICC-CNT)*, pages 1–6. IEEE.

Vignesh Radhakrishnan, Christina Joseph, and K Chandrasekaran. 2018. Sentiment extraction from naturalistic video. *Procedia computer science*, 143:626–634.

Vikrant Somant and Amal Madan. 2015. Social signaling: Predicting the outcome of job interviews from vocal tone and prosody. In *Proceedings of the 2015 International Conference on Affective Computing and Intelligent Interaction (ACII)*, ACII '15, pages 139–145, Washington, DC, USA. IEEE Computer Society.

David Thissen, Lynne Steinberg, and Daniel Kuang. 2002. Quick and easy implementation of the benjamini-hochberg procedure for controlling the false positive rate in multiple comparisons. *Journal of educational and behavioral statistics*, 27(1):77–83.

Alessandro Vinciarelli and Gelareh Mohammadi. 2014. A survey of personality computing. *IEEE Transactions on Affective Computing*, 5(3):273–291.

Amir Zadeh, Rowan Zellers, Eli Pincus, and Louis-Philippe Morency. 2016. Multimodal sentiment intensity analysis in videos: Facial gestures and verbal messages. *IEEE Intelligent Systems*, 31(6):82–88.

Audio-Visual Understanding of Passenger Intents
for In-Cabin Conversational Agents

Eda Okur   **Shachi H Kumar**   **Saurav Sahay**   **Lama Nachman**

Intel Labs, Anticipatory Computing Lab, USA

{eda.okur, shachi.h.kumar, saurav.sahay, lama.nachman}@intel.com

Abstract

Building multimodal dialogue understanding capabilities situated in the in-cabin context is crucial to enhance passenger comfort in autonomous vehicle (AV) interaction systems. To this end, understanding passenger intents from spoken interactions and vehicle vision systems is an important building block for developing contextual and visually grounded conversational agents for AV. Towards this goal, we explore AMIE (Automated-vehicle Multimodal In-cabin Experience), the in-cabin agent responsible for handling multimodal passenger-vehicle interactions. In this work, we discuss the benefits of multimodal understanding of in-cabin utterances by incorporating verbal/language input together with the non-verbal/acoustic and visual input from inside and outside the vehicle. Our experimental results outperformed text-only baselines as we achieved improved performances for intent detection with multimodal approach.

1   Introduction

Understanding passenger intents from spoken interactions and visual cues (both from inside and outside the vehicle) is an important building block towards developing contextual and scene-aware dialogue systems for autonomous vehicles. When the passengers give instructions to the in-cabin agent AMIE, the agent should parse commands properly considering three modalities (i.e., verbal/language/text, vocal/audio, visual/video) and trigger the appropriate functionality of the AV system.

For in-cabin dialogue between car assistants and driver/passengers, recent studies explore creating a public dataset using a WoZ approach (Eric et al., 2017) and improving ASR for passenger speech recognition (Fukui et al., 2018). Another recent work (Zheng et al., 2017) attempts to classify sentences as navigation-related or not using the

CU-Move in-vehicle speech corpus (Hansen et al., 2001), a relatively old and large corpus focusing on route navigation.

We collected a multimodal in-cabin dataset with multi-turn dialogues between the passengers and AMIE using a Wizard-of-Oz (WoZ) scheme via realistic scavenger hunt game. In previous work (Okur et al., 2019), we experimented with various RNN-based models to detect the utterance-level intents (i.e., *set-destination, change-route, go-faster, go-slower, stop, park, pull-over, drop-off, open-door, other*) along with the intent keywords and relevant slots (i.e., *location, position/direction, object, gesture/gaze, time-guidance, person*) associated with these intents.

In this work, we discuss the benefits of a multimodal understanding of in-cabin utterances by incorporating verbal/language input together with the non-verbal/acoustic and visual cues, both from inside and outside the vehicle (e.g., passenger gestures and gaze from in-cabin video stream, referred objects outside of the vehicle from the road view camera stream).

2   Data

Our AMIE in-cabin dataset includes 30 hours of multimodal data collected from 30 passengers (15 female, 15 male) in a total of 20 sessions. In 10 sessions, a single passenger was present, whereas the remaining 10 sessions include two passengers interacting with the vehicle. Participants sit in the back of the vehicle, separated from the driver and the human acting as an agent at the front. The vehicle is modified to hide the operator and the WoZ AMIE agent from the passengers, using a variation of the WoZ approach (Wang et al., 2017). In each ride/session, which lasted about 1 hour or more, the participants were playing a realistic scavenger hunt game on the streets of Richmond, BC,

Proceedings of the 58th Annual Meeting of the Association for Computational Linguistics, pages 55–59

Seattle, USA, July5 - 10, 2020. ©2017 Association for Computational Linguistics

https://doi.org/10.18653/v1/P17

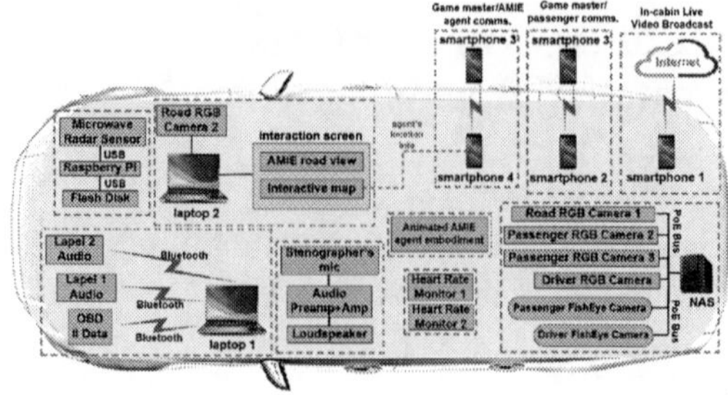

Figure 1: AMIE In-cabin Data Collection Setup

Canada. Passengers treat the vehicle as AV and communicate with the WoZ AMIE agent mainly via speech commands. Game objectives require passengers to interact naturally with the agent to go to certain destinations, update routes, give specific directions regarding where to pull over or park (sometimes with gestures), find landmarks (refer to outside objects), stop the vehicle, change speed, get in and out of the vehicle, etc. Further details of the data collection protocol and dataset statistics can be found in (Sherry et al., 2018; Okur et al., 2019). See Fig. 1 for the vehicle instrumentation to enable multimodal data collection setup.

2.1 Dataset Statistics

Multimodal AMIE dataset consists of in-cabin conversations between the passengers and the AV agent, with 10590 utterances in total. 1331 of these utterances have commands to the WoZ agent, hence they are associated with passenger intents. Utterance-level intent and word-level slot annotations are obtained on the transcribed utterances by majority voting of 3 annotators. The annotation results for *utterance-level intent* types, *slots* and *intent keywords* can be found in Table 1 and Table 2.

3 Methodology

We explored leveraging multimodality for the Natural Language Understanding (NLU) module in the Spoken Dialogue System (SDS) pipeline. As our AMIE in-cabin dataset has audio and video recordings, we investigated three modalities for the NLU: text, audio, and visual.

For text (verbal/language) modality, we employed the Hierarchical & Joint Bi-LSTM model (Schuster and Paliwal, 1997; Hakkani-Tur et al., 2016; Zhang and Wang, 2016; Wen et al., 2018), namely H-Joint-2.

- **Hierarchical & Joint Model (H-Joint-2)**: This is a 2-level hierarchical joint learning model that detects/extracts *intent keywords* & *slots* using sequence-to-sequence Bi-LSTMs first (Level-1), then only the words that are predicted as *intent keywords* & *valid slots* are fed into the Joint-2 model (Level-2), which is another sequence-to-sequence Bi-LSTM network for *utterance-level intent* detection, jointly trained with *slots* & *intent keywords*.

This architecture was chosen based on the best-performing uni-modal results presented in previous work (Okur et al., 2019) for utterance-level intent recognition and slot filling on our AMIE dataset. These initial uni-modal results were obtained on the transcribed text with pre-trained GloVe word embeddings (Pennington et al., 2014).

In this study, we explore the following multimodal features to better assess passenger intents for conversational agents in self-driving cars: word embeddings for text, speech embeddings and acoustic features for audio, and visual features for the video modality.

AMIE Scenario	Intent Type	Utterance Count
Set/Change Destination/Route	SetDestination	311
	SetRoute	507
Finishing the Trip	Park	151
	PullOver	34
	Stop	27
Set/Change Driving Behavior/Speed	GoFaster	73
	GoSlower	41
Others (Door, Music, A/C, etc.)	OpenDoor	136
	Other	51
	Total	*1331*

Table 1: AMIE In-cabin Dataset Statistics: Intents

Slot/Keyword Type	Word Count
Intent Keyword	2007
Location	1969
Position/Direction	1131
Person	404
Time Guidance	246
Gesture/Gaze	167
Object	110
None	6512
Total	*12546*

Table 2: AMIE In-cabin Dataset Statistics: Slots

Modalities	Features	F1(%)
Text	Word2Vec (37.6K vocab)	85.63
Text	GloVe (400K vocab)	89.02
Text & Audio	GloVe & Acoustic (openSMILE/IS10)	89.53
Text & Visual	GloVe & Video_cabin (CNN/Inception-ResNet)	89.40
Text & Visual	GloVe & Video_road (CNN/Inception-ResNet)	89.37
Text & Visual	GloVe & Video_cabin+road (CNN/Inception-ResNet)	89.68
Audio	Speech2Vec (37.6K vocab)	84.47
Text & Audio	Word2Vec+Speech2Vec	88.08
Text & Audio	GloVe+Speech2Vec	90.85
Text & Audio	GloVe+Word2Vec+Speech2Vec	91.29
Text & Audio	GloVe+Word2Vec+Speech2Vec & Acoustic (IS10)	91.68
Text & Audio & Visual	GloVe+Word2Vec+Speech2Vec & Video_cabin (CNN)	91.50
Text & Audio & Visual	GloVe+Word2Vec+Speech2Vec & Video_cabin+road (CNN)	91.55

Table 3: F1-scores of Intent Recognition with Multimodal Features

3.1 Word and Speech Embeddings

We incorporated pre-trained speech embeddings, called Speech2Vec[1], as additional audio-related features. These Speech2Vec embeddings (Chung and Glass, 2018) are trained on a corpus of 500 hours of speech from LibriSpeech. Speech2Vec can be considered as a speech version of Word2Vec embeddings (Mikolov et al., 2013), where the idea is that learning the representations directly from speech can capture the information carried by speech that may not exist in plain text.

We experimented with concatenating word and speech vectors using GloVe embeddings (6B tokens, 400K vocab, 100-dim), Speech2Vec embeddings (37.6K vocab, 100-dim), and its Word2Vec (37.6K vocab, 100-dim) counterpart, in which the Word2Vec embeddings are trained on the transcript of the same LibriSpeech corpus.

3.2 Acoustic Features

Using openSMILE[2] audio feature extraction toolkit (Eyben et al., 2013), 1582 acoustic features are extracted for each utterance using the segmented audio clips from AMIE dataset. These are the INTERSPEECH 2010 Paralinguistic Challenge (IS10) features (Schuller et al., 2010) including PCM (pulse-code modulation) loudness, MFCC (Mel-frequency cepstral coefficients), log Mel Freq. Band, LSP (line spectral pairs) Frequency, etc.

3.3 Visual Features

Intermediate CNN features[3] are extracted from each video clip segmented per utterance from the AMIE dataset. Using the feature extraction process described in (Kordopatis-Zilos et al., 2017), one frame per second is sampled for any given input video clip and its visual descriptors are extracted from the activations of the intermediate convolution layers of a pre-trained CNN. We used the pre-trained Inception-ResNet-v2 model[4] (Szegedy et al., 2016) and generated 4096-dim features for each sample. We experimented with utilizing two sources of visual information: (i) cabin/passenger view from the back-driver RGB camera recordings, (ii) road/outside view from the dash-cam RGB video streams.

4 Experimental Results

Performance results of the utterance-level intent recognition models with varying modality and feature concatenations can be found in Table 3, using hierarchical joint learning (H-Joint-2). For text and speech embeddings experiments, we observe that using Word2Vec or Speech2Vec representations achieve comparable F1-score performances, which are significantly below the GloVe embeddings performance. This was expected as the pre-trained Speech2Vec vectors have lower vocabulary coverage than the GloVe vectors. On the

---

[1]`https://github.com/iamyuanchung/speech2vec-pretrained-vectors`
[2]`https://www.audeering.com/opensmile/`
[3]`https://github.com/MKLab-ITI/intermediate-cnn-features`
[4]`https://github.com/tensorflow/models/tree/master/research/slim`

other hand, we observe that concatenating GloVe + Speech2Vec embeddings, and further GloVe + Word2Vec + Speech2Vec yields higher F1-scores for intent recognition. These results show that the speech embeddings indeed can capture useful semantic information carried by speech only, which may not exist in plain text.

We also investigate incorporating the audio-visual features on top of text-only and text + speech embedding models. Including openSMILE/IS10 acoustic features from audio as well as intermediate CNN/Inception-ResNet-v2 features from video brings slight improvements to our intent recognition models, achieving 0.92 F1-score. These initial results may require further explorations for specific intents such as *stop* (e.g., audio intensity & loudness could have helped), or for relevant slots such as passenger *gesture/gaze* (e.g., cabin-view features) and outside *object*s (e.g., road-view features).

5   Conclusion and Future Work

In this work, we briefly present our initial explorations towards the multimodal understanding of passenger utterances in autonomous vehicles. We show that our experimental results outperformed the uni-modal text-only baseline results, and with multimodality, we achieved improved performances for passenger intent detection in AV. This ongoing research has the potential impact of exploring real-world challenges with human-vehicle-scene interactions for autonomous driving support via spoken utterances.

There exist various exciting recent work on improved multimodal fusion techniques (Zadeh et al., 2018; Liang et al., 2019a; Pham et al., 2019; Baltrušaitis et al., 2019). In addition to the simplified feature and modality concatenations, we plan to explore some of these promising tensor-based multimodal fusion networks (Liu et al., 2018; Liang et al., 2019b; Tsai et al., 2019) for more robust intent classification on AMIE dataset as future work.

References

T. Baltrušaitis, C. Ahuja, and L. Morency. 2019. Multimodal machine learning: A survey and taxonomy. *IEEE Transactions on Pattern Analysis and Machine Intelligence*, 41(2):423–443.

Yu-An Chung and James Glass. 2018. Speech2vec: A sequence-to-sequence framework for learning word embeddings from speech. In *Proc. INTERSPEECH 2018*, pages 811–815.

Mihail Eric, Lakshmi Krishnan, Francois Charette, and Christopher D. Manning. 2017. Key-value retrieval networks for task-oriented dialogue. In *Proceedings of the 18th Annual SIGdial Meeting on Discourse and Dialogue*, pages 37–49. Association for Computational Linguistics.

Florian Eyben, Felix Weninger, Florian Gross, and Björn Schuller. 2013. Recent developments in opensmile, the munich open-source multimedia feature extractor. In *Proc. ACM International Conference on Multimedia*, MM '13, pages 835–838.

M. Fukui, T. Watanabe, and M. Kanazawa. 2018. Sound source separation for plural passenger speech recognition in smart mobility system. *IEEE Transactions on Consumer Electronics*, 64(3):399–405.

Dilek Hakkani-Tur, Gokhan Tur, Asli Celikyilmaz, Yun-Nung Vivian Chen, Jianfeng Gao, Li Deng, and Ye-Yi Wang. 2016. Multi-domain joint semantic frame parsing using bi-directional rnn-lstm. ISCA.

John HL Hansen, Pongtep Angkititrakul, Jay Plucienkowski, Stephen Gallant, Umit Yapanel, Bryan Pellom, Wayne Ward, and Ron Cole. 2001. Cumove: Analysis & corpus development for interactive in-vehicle speech systems. In *Seventh European Conference on Speech Communication and Technology*.

Giorgos Kordopatis-Zilos, Symeon Papadopoulos, Ioannis Patras, and Yiannis Kompatsiaris. 2017. Near-duplicate video retrieval by aggregating intermediate cnn layers. In *International Conference on Multimedia Modeling*, pages 251–263. Springer.

Paul Pu Liang, Yao Chong Lim, Yao-Hung Hubert Tsai, Ruslan Salakhutdinov, and Louis-Philippe Morency. 2019a. Strong and simple baselines for multimodal utterance embeddings. In *Proceedings of the 2019 Conference of the North American Chapter of the Association for Computational Linguistics: Human Language Technologies, Volume 1 (Long and Short Papers)*, pages 2599–2609, Minneapolis, Minnesota. Association for Computational Linguistics.

Paul Pu Liang, Zhun Liu, Yao-Hung Hubert Tsai, Qibin Zhao, Ruslan Salakhutdinov, and Louis-Philippe Morency. 2019b. Learning representations from imperfect time series data via tensor rank regularization. In *Proceedings of the 57th Annual Meeting of the Association for Computational Linguistics*, pages 1569–1576, Florence, Italy. Association for Computational Linguistics.

Zhun Liu, Ying Shen, Varun Bharadhwaj Lakshminarasimhan, Paul Pu Liang, AmirAli Bagher Zadeh, and Louis-Philippe Morency. 2018. Efficient low-rank multimodal fusion with modality-specific factors. *Proceedings of the 56th Annual Meeting of the Association for Computational Linguistics (Volume 1: Long Papers)*.

Tomas Mikolov, Ilya Sutskever, Kai Chen, Greg Corrado, and Jeffrey Dean. 2013. Distributed representations of words and phrases and their compositionality. In *Proceedings of the 26th International Conference on Neural Information Processing Systems - Volume 2*, NIPS'13, pages 3111–3119, USA.

Eda Okur, Shachi H Kumar, Saurav Sahay, Asli Arslan Esme, and Lama Nachman. 2019. Natural language interactions in autonomous vehicles: Intent detection and slot filling from passenger utterances. *20th International Conference on Computational Linguistics and Intelligent Text Processing (CICLing 2019)*.

Jeffrey Pennington, Richard Socher, and Christopher D. Manning. 2014. Glove: Global vectors for word representation. In *Empirical Methods in Natural Language Processing (EMNLP'14)*.

Hai Pham, Paul Pu Liang, Thomas Manzini, Louis-Philippe Morency, and Barnabás Póczos. 2019. Found in translation: Learning robust joint representations by cyclic translations between modalities. In *Proceedings of the AAAI Conference on Artificial Intelligence*, volume 33, pages 6892–6899.

Björn Schuller, Stefan Steidl, Anton Batliner, Felix Burkhardt, Laurence Devillers, Christian Müller, and Shrikanth S Narayanan. 2010. The interspeech 2010 paralinguistic challenge. In *Proc. INTER-SPEECH 2010*.

M. Schuster and K.K. Paliwal. 1997. Bidirectional recurrent neural networks. *Trans. Sig. Proc.*, 45(11):2673–2681.

John Sherry, Richard Beckwith, Asli Arslan Esme, and Cagri Tanriover. 2018. Getting things done in an autonomous vehicle. In *Social Robots in the Wild Workshop, 13th ACM/IEEE International Conference on Human-Robot Interaction (HRI 2018)*.

Christian Szegedy, Sergey Ioffe, and Vincent Vanhoucke. 2016. Inception-v4, inception-resnet and the impact of residual connections on learning. *CoRR*, abs/1602.07261.

Yao-Hung Hubert Tsai, Shaojie Bai, Paul Pu Liang, J. Zico Kolter, Louis-Philippe Morency, and Ruslan Salakhutdinov. 2019. Multimodal transformer for unaligned multimodal language sequences. In *Proceedings of the 57th Annual Meeting of the Association for Computational Linguistics (Volume 1: Long Papers)*, Florence, Italy. Association for Computational Linguistics.

Peter Wang, Srinath Sibi, Brian Mok, and Wendy Ju. 2017. Marionette: Enabling on-road wizard-of-oz autonomous driving studies. In *Proceedings of the 2017 ACM/IEEE International Conference on Human-Robot Interaction*, HRI '17, pages 234–243, New York, NY, USA. ACM.

Liyun Wen, Xiaojie Wang, Zhenjiang Dong, and Hong Chen. 2018. Jointly modeling intent identification and slot filling with contextual and hierarchical information. In *Natural Language Processing and Chinese Computing*, pages 3–15, Cham. Springer.

Amir Zadeh, Paul Pu Liang, Navonil Mazumder, Soujanya Poria, Erik Cambria, and Louis-Philippe Morency. 2018. Memory fusion network for multi-view sequential learning. *Proceedings of the Thirty-Second AAAI Conference on Artificial Intelligence*.

Xiaodong Zhang and Houfeng Wang. 2016. A joint model of intent determination and slot filling for spoken language understanding. In *Proceedings of the Twenty-Fifth International Joint Conference on Artificial Intelligence*, IJCAI'16, pages 2993–2999.

Y. Zheng, Y. Liu, and J. H. L. Hansen. 2017. Navigation-orientated natural spoken language understanding for intelligent vehicle dialogue. In *2017 IEEE Intelligent Vehicles Symposium (IV)*, pages 559–564.

AI Sensing for Robotics using Deep Learning based Visual and Language Modeling

Yuvaram Singh
HCL Technologies Limited,
Analytics CoE
Noida, India, 201304
yuvaramsingh94@gmail.com

Kameshwar Rao JV
HCL Technologies Limited,
Analytics CoE
Noida, India, 201304
kameshjvkr@gmail.com

Abstract

An artificial intelligence(AI) system should be capable of processing the sensory inputs to extract both task-specific and general information about its environment. However, most of the existing algorithms extract only task specific information. In this work, an innovative approach to address the problem of processing visual sensory data is presented by utilizing convolutional neural network (CNN). It recognizes and represents the physical and semantic nature of the surrounding in both human readable and machine processable format. This work utilizes the image captioning model to capture the semantics of the input image and a modular design to generate a probability distribution for semantic topics. It gives any autonomous system the ability to process visual information in a human-like way and generates more insights which are hardly possible with a conventional algorithm. Here a model and data collection method are proposed.

1 Introduction

In a world gifted with visible light facilitating information sharing, the living creatures have developed organs for sensing the light to understand their surrounding. In an autonomous system, this information is captured in IR, UV, and visible spectrum involving sophisticated sensors and is processed using complex algorithms. At Consumer Electronics Show (CES) 2020, Samsung presented Ballie which is a personalized robot with ideas to make it self-aware of its surroundings and control IoT devices around home to make the environment better. With companies targeting to launch smart home robots with capabilities of following voice commands, there is a need to develop a system that can automatically understand the semantics of the environment and take appropriate decisions on its own.

(a) a person cutting cake while others cheering. (b) Fire fighters are trying to put out fire in the building.

Figure 1: Variety of scenarios that a human can describe comfortably.

The latest work in scene understanding involved construction of knowledge graph for visual semantic understanding(Jiang et al., 2019). The authors used ontology graph in combination with visual captioning to describe the scene. Another approach for functional scene understanding was introduced using semantic segmentation(Wald et al., 2018). All these scene understanding approaches make a system specialized in certain tasks and working environment while failing to generalize across various types of situations and capture the human emotions.

It is efficient to make decision, based on a structured description of the scene instead of working on raw pixel information. Fig.1 shows scenarios where a human can easily interpret the meaning of the scene. It is easy to tell from the Fig.1b that firefighters are trying to put out the fire from building. This is also true for all the Fig.1a, 1b where a human can understand and explain the scene easily through a language representation.

In this work we recommend an AI sensing system that can semantically interpret the environmental conditions, objects, relations and activity carried out from the visual feed. These interpretations are converted into text for human understanding and probability distribution for the control system to process and take decisions. The main intention of this work is to have a neural network based sen-

Proceedings of the 58th Annual Meeting of the Association for Computational Linguistics, pages 60–63
Seattle, USA, July5 - 10, 2020. ©2017 Association for Computational Linguistics
https://doi.org/10.18653/v1/P17

sor processing unit capable of extracting semantic context while deployed on low powered compute hardware.

This paper is divided as follows:

- Section 2 explains various modules of the proposed approach.

- Section 3 discusses about the dataset and considerations to make while implementing this approach.

2 Proposed Approach

In this work, a modular approach is proposed to represent the semantic content of the outside world through vision sensor. A detailed flow diagram of the proposed method is shown in Fig.2. It consist of three sub-modules namely, CNN feature extractor, language module, and environment context probability detector module. It combines visual, language, and context detection modules to assist the control unit to make decisions based on non-task specific environment details.

2.1 CNN Feature Extractor

This module process the visual feed and convert them into feature tensor(f) which is used to generate semantic understanding of the surrounding. This feature tensor(f) encodes the information present in the incoming frame. A CNN based feature extractor(Xu et al., 2015) trained for image classification task on Imagenet dataset(Deng et al., 2009) is used. There are variety of CNN based pre-trained architectures are available to be used as feature extractors. Architectures such as Mobilenet(Sandler et al., 2018), ResNet(He et al., 2016), InceptionNet(Szegedy et al., 2015) and DenseNet(Huang et al., 2017) have their own benefits and drawbacks. Based on the deployment hardware, expected response time and environment nature, specific architecture can be chosen.

2.2 Language Module

In this module, the information from the feature tensor(f) are extracted and represented in a human interpretable language(l). This is achieved by using Long Short Term Memory unit(LSTM)(Sak et al., 2014) which is a deep neural network(DNN) for generating sequential output(Xu et al., 2015). A combination of soft-attention mechanism(Xu et al., 2015) and LSTM is used to describe the contents extracted from the frame(Vinodababu, 2018). This

is a recursive step where the execution comes to a halt when the end token $< end >$ is predicted or maximum sentence length is reached.

$$l = \{w_0, w_1, w_2, ...w_n\}$$

where

$$w_i \in R^k$$

Here R^k is the vector of tokenized words in the vocabulary and (l) is the generated word sequence. The byproduct of having language representation is explainability of action.

The process of caption generation happens recursively were to sample a word w from R^k it goes through the following process. Ref Fig.3.

At a time step t,

- The attention mechanism computes the mask m_t for feature tensor$f$ using f and hidden state H_{t-1}.

- f weighted by m_t combined with the previous word detected w_{t-1} is passed onto the LSTM along with hidden state H_{t-1} and cell state C_{t-1} from the previous step.

- The LSTM output a probability distribution for the words in the vocabulary R.

This process is carried out until the end token $< end >$ is predicted or the max length of caption is reached. The effectiveness of this module depends on generation of dense caption for the scene.

2.3 Environment Context Detector

The verbal representation from language module is used to generate probability distribution over various groups of semantic context. The input sequence is tokanized, vectorized and converted into probability distribution by using fully connected network. It is constructed by single or multiple neural net operating parallel, perform prediction over various context. Fig.4 provides the overall view of this module where different fully connected network(FCN) are used for prediction. The caption are tokanized and vectorized to act as input. Here GloVe embedding(Pennington et al., 2014) is used to vectorize the sentence. The activation of the output layer can use either softmax or sigmoid based on the nature of the data. The topics of the context should be decided based on the workspace and

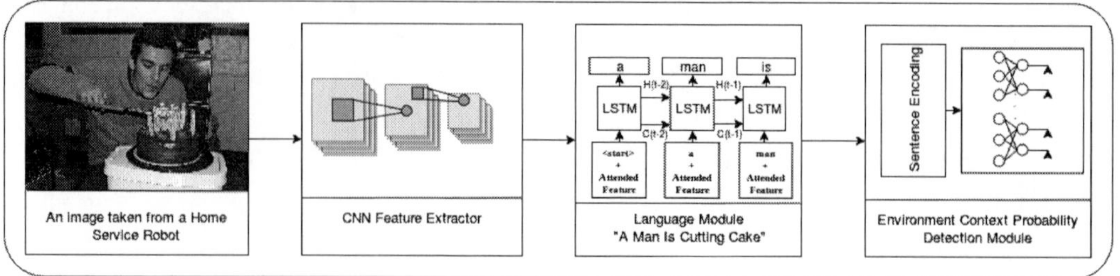

Figure 2: A block diagram of the proposed model.

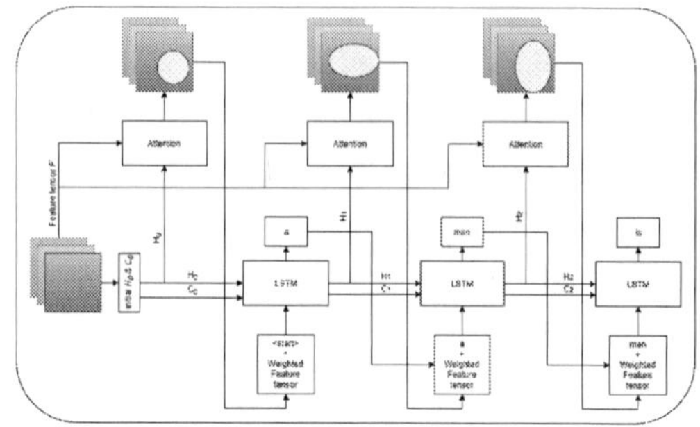

Figure 3: A flow diagram explaining how language module prediction the next word in sequence.(Xu et al., 2015)

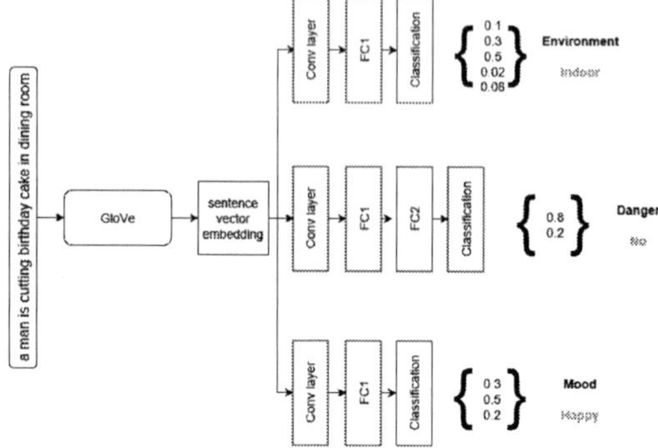

Figure 4: A block diagram of environment context detector.

preference of the robotics designer. Fig.4, shows environment context detector block diagram.

$$\mathbf{E} = [c_0, c_1, ... c_d]$$

where c_i is the prediction vector of ith context net and $\mathbf{E}$ is the collection of c vectors. Here d is the desired number of context net. The generated probability distribution is sent to the control system which takes the final decision whether to react or not. The proposed solution serves as an add-on to the existing control system.

3 Dataset and Considerations

The CNN feature extractor is a pre-trained model trained on Imagenet dataset(Deng et al., 2009) for classifying 1000 objects. The language module is trained using COCO image captioning dataset(Lin et al., 2014) which consist of image and captions in target language. A BLEU-1 score of 70.7 is achieved for the language module.

The dataset for the environment context module is similar to the text sentiment classification dataset. The input will be a sentence and the labels are one-hot vector of target class. A dataset is created from a portion of COCO caption where the

semantic context topics are environment, situation, mood, presence of human, and objects in the scene as shown in Fig.4. There are several logical considerations to be take while adopting this method. few of them are,

- On board compute capability to carryout DNN calculation.

- Robot deployment environment and its nature.

- The actual intention and task of the robot.

- How the control system should react to the generated probability distribution.

4 Conclusion

The main objective of the work is to use neural networks to understand and represent the physical environment around the system. This work serve as an add-on to the existing control system by providing additional set of inputs capturing the semantic meaning. An image captioning based approach is used to obtain semantic content of the surrounding and it is represented in a probability distribution.

References

J. Deng, W. Dong, R. Socher, L.-J. Li, K. Li, and L. Fei-Fei. 2009. ImageNet: A Large-Scale Hierarchical Image Database. In *CVPR09*.

Kaiming He, Xiangyu Zhang, Shaoqing Ren, and Jian Sun. 2016. Deep residual learning for image recognition. In *Proceedings of the IEEE conference on computer vision and pattern recognition*, pages 770–778.

Gao Huang, Zhuang Liu, Laurens Van Der Maaten, and Kilian Q Weinberger. 2017. Densely connected convolutional networks. In *Proceedings of the IEEE conference on computer vision and pattern recognition*, pages 4700–4708.

Chen Jiang, Steven Lu, and Martin Jagersand. 2019. Constructing dynamic knowledge graph for visual semantic understanding and applications in autonomous robotics. *arXiv preprint arXiv:1909.07459*.

Tsung-Yi Lin, Michael Maire, Serge Belongie, James Hays, Pietro Perona, Deva Ramanan, Piotr Dollár, and C Lawrence Zitnick. 2014. Microsoft coco: Common objects in context. In *European conference on computer vision*, pages 740–755. Springer.

Jeffrey Pennington, Richard Socher, and Christopher D. Manning. 2014. Glove: Global vectors for word representation. In *Empirical Methods in Natural Language Processing (EMNLP)*, pages 1532–1543.

Haşim Sak, Andrew Senior, and Françoise Beaufays. 2014. Long short-term memory recurrent neural network architectures for large scale acoustic modeling. In *Fifteenth annual conference of the international speech communication association*.

Mark Sandler, Andrew Howard, Menglong Zhu, Andrey Zhmoginov, and Liang-Chieh Chen. 2018. Mobilenetv2: Inverted residuals and linear bottlenecks. In *Proceedings of the IEEE Conference on Computer Vision and Pattern Recognition*, pages 4510–4520.

Christian Szegedy, Wei Liu, Yangqing Jia, Pierre Sermanet, Scott Reed, Dragomir Anguelov, Dumitru Erhan, Vincent Vanhoucke, and Andrew Rabinovich. 2015. Going deeper with convolutions. In *Proceedings of the IEEE conference on computer vision and pattern recognition*, pages 1–9.

Sagar Vinodababu. 2018. a-pytorch-tutorial-to-image-captioning. https://github.com/sgrvinod/a-PyTorch-Tutorial-to-Image-Captioning.

Johanna Wald, Keisuke Tateno, Jürgen Sturm, Nassir Navab, and Federico Tombari. 2018. Real-time fully incremental scene understanding on mobile platforms. *IEEE Robotics and Automation Letters*, 3(4):3402–3409.

Kelvin Xu, Jimmy Ba, Ryan Kiros, Kyunghyun Cho, Aaron Courville, Ruslan Salakhudinov, Rich Zemel, and Yoshua Bengio. 2015. Show, attend and tell: Neural image caption generation with visual attention. In *International conference on machine learning*, pages 2048–2057.

Exploring Weaknesses of VQA Models through Attribution Driven Insights

Shaunak Halbe

College of Engineering Pune

shaunak9@ieee.org

Abstract

Deep Neural Networks have been successfully used for the task of Visual Question Answering for the past few years owing to the availability of relevant large scale datasets. However these datasets are created in artificial settings and rarely reflect the real world scenario. Recent research effectively applies these VQA models for answering visual questions for the blind. Despite achieving high accuracy these models appear to be susceptible to variation in input questions.We analyze popular VQA models through the lens of attribution (input's influence on predictions) to gain valuable insights. Further, We use these insights to craft adversarial attacks which inflict significant damage to these systems with negligible change in meaning of the input questions. We believe this will enhance development of systems more robust to the possible variations in inputs when deployed to assist the visually impaired.

1   Introduction

Visual Question Answering (VQA) is a semantic task, where a model attempts to answer a natural language question based on the visual context. With the emergence of large scale datasets (Antol et al., 2015; Goyal et al., 2017; Krishna et al., 2016; Malinowski and Fritz, 2014; Zhu et al., 2016), There has been outstanding progress in VQA systems in terms of accuracy obtained on the associated test sets. However these systems are seen to somewhat fail when applied in real-world situations (Gurari et al., 2018; Agrawal et al., 2016) majorly due to a significant domain shift and an inherent language/image bias. A direct application of VQA is to answer the questions for images captured by blind people. The VizWiz (Gurari et al., 2018) is a first of its kind goal oriented dataset which reflects the challenges conventional VQA models might face when applied to assist the blind. The questions

in this dataset are not straightforward and are often conversational which is natural knowing that they have been asked by visually impaired people for assistance. Due to unsuitable images or irrelevant questions most of these questions are unanswerable. These questions differ from those in other datasets mainly in the type of answer they are expecting. The questions are often subjective and require the algorithm to actually read (OCR)/ detect/ count, moreover understand the image before answering. We believe models trained on such a challenging dataset must be interpretable and should be analyzed for robustness to ensure they are accurate for the right reasons.

2   Model Interpretability

Deep Neural Networks often lack interpretability but are widely used owing to their high accuracy on the representative test sets. In most applications a high test-set accuracy is sufficient, but in certain sensitive areas, understanding causality is crucial. When deploying such VQA models to aid the blind, utmost care needs to be taken to prevent the model from answering wrongly to avoid possible accidents. In the past, various saliency methods have been used to interpret models which have textual inputs. Vanilla Gradient Method(Simonyan et al., 2013) visualizes the gradients of the loss with respect to each input token(word in this case). SmoothGrad (Smilkov et al., 2017) averages the gradient by adding Gaussian noise to the input. Layerwise Relevance Propagation (LRP) (Binder et al., 2016), DeepLift (Shrikumar et al., 2017) are similar methods used for this purpose.

3   Integrated Gradients (IG)

Vanilla, LRP and DeepLift violate the axioms of Sensitivity and Implementational Invariance as discussed by Sundararajan et al. 2017. As Integrated

Proceedings of the 58th Annual Meeting of the Association for Computational Linguistics, pages 64–68
Seattle, USA, July5 - 10, 2020. ©2017 Association for Computational Linguistics
https://doi.org/10.18653/v1/P17

Gradients (IG)(Sundararajan et al., 2017) satisfies the necessary axioms, we use it for the purpose of interpretability. IG computes attributions for the input features based on the network's predictions. These attributions assign credit/blame to the input features (pixels in case of an image and words in case of a question) which are responsible for the output of the model. These attributions can help identify when a model is accurate for the wrong reasons like over-reliance on images or possible language priors. These attributions are computed with respect to a baseline input. In this paper, we use an empty question as the baseline. We use these attributions which specify word importance in the input question to design adversarial questions, which the model fails to answer correctly. While doing so, we try to preserve the original meaning of the question and ensure the simplicity of the same. We design these questions manually by incorporating highly attributed content-free words in the original question,taking into consideration the free-formed conversational nature of the questions that any user of such a system might ask. By content-free, we refer to words that are context independent like prepositions (e.g., "on", "in"), determiners (e.g., "this", "that") and certain qualifiers (e.g., "much", "many") among others.

4 Related Work

The main idea of adversarial attacks is to carefully perturb the input without making perceivable changes, in order to affect the prediction of the model. There has been significant research on adversarial attacks concerning images(Goodfellow et al., 2014; Madry et al., 2017). These attacks exploit the oversensitivity of models towards changes in the input image. Sharma et al. 2018 study attention guided implementations of popular image-based attacks on VQA models. Xu et al. 2018 discuss methods to generate targeted attacks to perturb input images in a multimodal setting. Ramakrishnan et al. 2018 observe that VQA models heavily rely on certain language priors to directly arrive at the answer irrespective of the image. They further develop a bias-reducing approach to improve performance. Kafle and Kanan 2017 study the response of VQA models towards various question categories to indicate the deficiencies in the datasets. Huang et al. 2019 analyze the robustness of VQA models on basic questions ranked on the basis of similarity by LASSO based optimization

method. Finally, Mudrakarta et al. 2018 use attributions to determine word importance and leverage them to craft adversarial questions. We adapt their ideas to the conversational aspect of questions in VizWiz to better suit our task. In this paper we restrict ourselves to attacks in the language domain, i.e. we only perturb the input questions and analyze the network's response.

5 Robustness Analysis

5.1 Model and Data Specifications

The VizWiz dataset (Gurari et al., 2018) consists of 20,523 training set image-question pairs and 4,319 validation pairs (Bhattacharya and Gurari, 2019). Whereas the VQA v2 dataset (Goyal et al., 2017) consists of 443,757 training questions and 214,354 validation questions. The VizWiz dataset is significantly smaller than other VQA datasets and hence is not ideal to determine word importance for the content free words. In order to do justice to these words and to keep the analysis generalizable we use the VQA v2 dataset for computing text attributions. We use the Counter model (Zhang et al., 2018) for the purpose of computing attributions. This model is structurally similar to the Q+I+A (Kazemi and Elqursh, 2017) (which was used to benchmark on VizWiz). We select this model for ease in reproducibility and for consistency with the original paper (Gurari et al., 2018). We compute attributions over the validation set, of which the highly attributed words are selected to design prefix and suffix phrases which can be incorporated in original questions for adversarial effect.Further we verify and test these attacks on the following models : (1) Pythia (Singh et al., 2019) (the VizWiz 2018 challenge winner) pretrained on VQA v2 and transferred to VizWiz (train split) and (2) Q+I+A model (which was used to benchmark on VizWiz) trained from scratch on VizWiz (train split).

5.2 Observations

We compute the total attribution that every word receives as well as average attribution for every word based on it's frequency of occurrence. We only take into account content free words, with the intention of preserving the meaning of the original question when these words are added to it. We observe that among the content-free words, 'what', 'many', 'is' 'this', 'how' consistently receive high attribution in a question. We use these words along with some other context independent words to de-

Figure 1: Attributions overlaid on the corresponding input words. The output of the model changes from 'yellow' to 1 which is driven by the word 'many'.

Figure 2: The output of the model is driven by the word 'answer' acting as an adversary.

sign the attacks. We use these words to create seemingly natural phrases to be prepended or appended to the question. We observe that the model alters it's prediction under the influence of these added words.

5.3 Suffix Attacks

We present Suffix Attacks, wherein we append content free phrases to the end of each question and evaluate the strength of these attacks through the accuracy obtained by the model on validation set and the percentage of answers it predicts as unanswerable/unsuitable (U).

5.4 Prefix Attacks

We expand the Prefix attacks of Mudrakarta et al. 2018 in a conversational vein to suit our task. These are seen to be more effective as prefix allows us to add important words like 'What' and 'How' to the start of a question which confuses the model to a greater extent than suffix attacks.

5.5 Evaluation and Analysis

The Pythia v3 (Singh et al., 2019) model achieves an accuracy of 53% while the Q+I+A model achieves 48.8% when evaluated on clean samples from the val-set. We tabulate the results obtained by using these phrases as prefixes and suffixes. It is worth noting that when tested on empty questions (which is the baseline for our task) Pythia retains an accuracy of 35.43% while Q+I+A retains 38.35%. Thus our strongest attacks which are meaningful combinations of the basic attacks(in bold; see Table 1 for Pythia) and (in bold; see Table 3 for Q+I+A) drop the model's accuracy close to the empty question lower bound. Our strongest attack (see Table 1) renders 97% of the questions unanswerable, which is a significant increase from 58% when evaluated on clean questions.

6 Performance on other attacks

6.1 Word Substitution

We observe that when we evaluate the model by substituting certain words of the input question by low-attributed words, which change the meaning of the question, the answer predicted in most cases

Pythia v0.3 (Singh et al., 2019)		
Prefix Phrase	Accuracy	% U
guide me on this	47.8	74.28
answer this for me	46.27	82.66
in not a lot of words	44.66	85.15
what is the answer to	43.46	86.10
in not many words	42.29	91.3
in not many words- what is the answer to	**38.16**	**97.06**

Table 1: Prefix attacks on Pythia v0.3

Pythia v0.3 (Singh et al., 2019)		
Suffix Phrase	Accuracy	% U
guide me on this	49.8	69.2
answer this for me	48.82	75.19
answer this for me- in not a lot of words	45.3	82.47
answer this for me- in not many words	**42.5**	**88.46**

Table 2: Suffix attacks on Pythia v0.3

Q+I+A (Kazemi and Elqursh, 2017)		
Suffix Phrase	Accuracy	% U
describe this for me	43.52	82.8
answer this for me	43.90	89.7
guide me on this	41.31	87.0
answer this for me- in not a lot of words	40.1	91.13
answer this for me- in not many words	**38.44**	**94.1**

Table 3: Suffix attacks on Q+I+A

Q+I+A (Kazemi and Elqursh, 2017)		
Prefix Phrase	Accuracy	% U
describe this for me	46.72	76.8
answer this for me	45.90	79.8
what is the answer to	44.72	80.6
in not many words	44.50	81.4
answer this for me- in not many words	**42.1**	**81.13**

Table 4: Prefix attacks on Q+I+A

is 'unanswerable'. This means that the model does not over-rely on images and is robust in this aspect.

6.2 Input Reduction

We follow the approach of Feng et al. 2018 to iteratively remove less important words from the input question. With the removal of around 50% words from a question, the accuracy drops close to 46% and renders 72% of the questions unanswerable. The Pythia model is fairly robust in this sense too, as it's output becomes 'unanswerable' after considerable input reduction.

6.3 Absurd Questions

To evaluate the effect of absurd attacks on these models, we make a short, non-exhaustive list of objects that do not appear in the validation set of VizWiz(questions, answers and captions) but are present in the training set. We use these objects to form questions similar to the training set questions which contained these objects. A good model should be able to detect absurd questions. For absurd questions like "which country's flag is this ?" (where "flag" does not occur in the validation set of VizWiz) Pythia predicts over 90% of these (clean image)-(absurd question) pairs as 'unanswerable' which is the desired outcome.

7 Conclusion

We analyzed two popular VQA models trained under different circumstances for robustness. Our analysis was driven by textual attributions, which helped identify shortcomings of the current approaches to solve a real world problem. The attacks discussed in this paper, illuminate the need for achieving robustness to scale up better to the task of visual assistance. To improve accessibility for the visually impaired, these VQA systems must be interpretable and safe for operation even under adverse conditions arising out of conversational variations. We believe these insights can be useful to surmount this challenging task.

References

Aishwarya Agrawal, Dhruv Batra, and Devi Parikh. 2016. Analyzing the behavior of visual question answering models. In *Proceedings of the 2016 Conference on Empirical Methods in Natural Language Processing*, pages 1955–1960, Austin, Texas. Association for Computational Linguistics.

Stanislaw Antol, Aishwarya Agrawal, Jiasen Lu, Margaret Mitchell, Dhruv Batra, C. Lawrence Zitnick, and Devi Parikh. 2015. VQA: Visual Question Answering. In *International Conference on Computer Vision (ICCV)*.

Nilavra Bhattacharya and Danna Gurari. 2019. Vizwiz dataset browser: A tool for visualizing machine learning datasets. *arXiv preprint arXiv:1912.09336*.

Alexander Binder, Grégoire Montavon, Sebastian Lapuschkin, Klaus-Robert Müller, and Wojciech Samek. 2016. Layer-wise relevance propagation for neural networks with local renormalization layers. In *International Conference on Artificial Neural Networks*, pages 63–71. Springer.

Shi Feng, Eric Wallace, II Grissom, Mohit Iyyer, Pedro Rodriguez, Jordan Boyd-Graber, et al. 2018. Pathologies of neural models make interpretations difficult. *arXiv preprint arXiv:1804.07781*.

Ian J Goodfellow, Jonathon Shlens, and Christian Szegedy. 2014. Explaining and harnessing adversarial examples. *arXiv preprint arXiv:1412.6572*.

Yash Goyal, Tejas Khot, Douglas Summers-Stay, Dhruv Batra, and Devi Parikh. 2017. Making the V in VQA matter: Elevating the role of image understanding in Visual Question Answering. In *Conference on Computer Vision and Pattern Recognition (CVPR)*.

Danna Gurari, Qing Li, Abigale J Stangl, Anhong Guo, Chi Lin, Kristen Grauman, Jiebo Luo, and Jeffrey P Bigham. 2018. Vizwiz grand challenge: Answering visual questions from blind people. *CVPR*.

Jia-Hong Huang, Cuong Duc Dao, Modar Alfadly, and Bernard Ghanem. 2019. A novel framework for robustness analysis of visual qa models. In *Proceedings of the AAAI Conference on Artificial Intelligence*, volume 33, pages 8449–8456.

Kushal Kafle and Christopher Kanan. 2017. An analysis of visual question answering algorithms. In *Proceedings of the IEEE International Conference on Computer Vision*, pages 1965–1973.

Vahid Kazemi and Ali Elqursh. 2017. Show, ask, attend, and answer: A strong baseline for visual question answering.

Ranjay Krishna, Yuke Zhu, Oliver Groth, Justin Johnson, Kenji Hata, Joshua Kravitz, Stephanie Chen, Yannis Kalantidis, Li-Jia Li, David A Shamma, Michael Bernstein, and Li Fei-Fei. 2016. Visual genome: Connecting language and vision using crowdsourced dense image annotations.

Aleksander Madry, Aleksandar Makelov, Ludwig Schmidt, Dimitris Tsipras, and Adrian Vladu. 2017. Towards deep learning models resistant to adversarial attacks. *arXiv preprint arXiv:1706.06083*.

Mateusz Malinowski and Mario Fritz. 2014. A multiworld approach to question answering about real-world scenes based on uncertain input. In *Advances in Neural Information Processing Systems 27*, pages 1682–1690. Curran Associates, Inc.

Pramod Kaushik Mudrakarta, Ankur Taly, Mukund Sundararajan, and Kedar Dhamdhere. 2018. Did the model understand the question? In *Proceedings of the 56th Annual Meeting of the Association for Computational Linguistics (Volume 1: Long Papers)*, pages 1896–1906, Melbourne, Australia. Association for Computational Linguistics.

Sainandan Ramakrishnan, Aishwarya Agrawal, and Stefan Lee. 2018. Overcoming language priors in visual question answering with adversarial regularization. In *Advances in Neural Information Processing Systems*, pages 1541–1551.

Vasu Sharma, Ankita Kalra, Vaibhav, Sumedha Chaudhary, Labhesh Patel, and Louis-Phillippe Morency. 2018. Attend and attack : Attention guided adversarial attacks on visual question answering models.

Avanti Shrikumar, Peyton Greenside, and Anshul Kundaje. 2017. Learning important features through propagating activation differences. In *Proceedings of the 34th International Conference on Machine Learning-Volume 70*, pages 3145–3153. JMLR. org.

Karen Simonyan, Andrea Vedaldi, and Andrew Zisserman. 2013. Deep inside convolutional networks: Visualising image classification models and saliency maps. *arXiv preprint arXiv:1312.6034*.

Amanpreet Singh, Vivek Natarajan, Yu Jiang, Xinlei Chen, Meet Shah, Marcus Rohrbach, Dhruv Batra, and Devi Parikh. 2019. Pythia-a platform for vision & language research. In *SysML Workshop, NeurIPS*, volume 2018.

Daniel Smilkov, Nikhil Thorat, Been Kim, Fernanda Viégas, and Martin Wattenberg. 2017. Smoothgrad: removing noise by adding noise. *arXiv preprint arXiv:1706.03825*.

Mukund Sundararajan, Ankur Taly, and Qiqi Yan. 2017. Axiomatic attribution for deep networks. In *Proceedings of the 34th International Conference on Machine Learning - Volume 70*, ICML'17, page 3319–3328. JMLR.org.

Xiaojun Xu, Xinyun Chen, Chang Liu, Anna Rohrbach, Trevor Darrell, and Dawn Song. 2018. Fooling vision and language models despite localization and attention mechanism. In *Proceedings of the IEEE Conference on Computer Vision and Pattern Recognition*, pages 4951–4961.

Yan Zhang, Jonathon Hare, and Adam Prügel-Bennett. 2018. Learning to count objects in natural images for visual question answering. In *International Conference on Learning Representations*.

Yuke Zhu, Oliver Groth, Michael Bernstein, and Li Fei-Fei. 2016. Visual7w: Grounded question answering in images. In *Proceedings of the IEEE conference on computer vision and pattern recognition*, pages 4995–5004.

Author Index